AF393378

Maher Asaad Baker

The Viking Legacy

ISBN Softcover: 978-3-384-16022-5
ISBN Hardback: 978-3-384-16023-2
ISBN Large print: 978-3-384-16025-6

CONTENTS

Introduction

In our modern, sedentary world of relative peace and stability, the ferocity and wanderlust of the Vikings seem almost unfathomable. For over three centuries, from the late 8th to the 11th century AD, bands of Scandinavian warriors known as Vikings terrorized Europe with their hit-and-run raids along coasts and navigable inland waterways. Sailing in sturdy longships ideally suited to shallow waters, the

Vikings - most prominently from modern-day Norway, Sweden, and Denmark - established settlements, traded, and Even amidst their reputation for violence, however, the Vikings also left an enduring cultural legacy across northern Europe and beyond. Their ambition and seamless adaptation to new environments demonstrated a pragmatic, entrepreneurial spirit ahead of their time. Amidst the turbulent circumstances of their Age, core Scandinavian virtues of courage, independence, fierce protectiveness of familial and community bonds, and reverence for skill, achievement, and honorable action found expression. Their saga encodes lessons that remain profoundly relevant to cultivating meaning, purpose, and psychological health amidst today's uncertainties.

To understand the Viking way of life, one must first comprehend the environmental circumstances that shaped it. Scandinavia consists primarily of mountainous regions, deep fjords, islands, and narrow habitable coastal strips - a landscape naturally isolating but rich in natural resources with seasons of immense contrast between perpetual night and constant summer sun. Such extremes fostered resilience and self-reliance in her people. Long, frigid winters required advanced preparation, communal cooperation, and storage of provisions - yet also allowed for extended periods of rest and contemplation sheltered from the elements.

The combination of rugged geography, seasonal challenges, and scarce arable land meant traditional Scandinavian societies organized along loose clan and kinship structures rather than expansive states. Allegiance centered on honor shared identity, and pragmatic alliances of mutual necessity rather than authorities distant and impersonal. This prized autonomy and cultivated a hardy, independent spirit that would serve Vikings so well upon the open sea and foreign shores. It also bred a fierce dedication to protecting one's own through strength of arms when needed. An individual's worth is derived not from titles or social status but competence, courage, and contributions to their community - virtues reflected in their poetic-prose traditions known as the "Eddas."

Scandinavia, nestled in the northeastern periphery of Europe, found itself in a unique position throughout history. This geographical location placed

Scandinavian societies at the crossroads of influential civilizations, both to the south and east. This advantageous position facilitated extensive trade networks, allowing Scandinavians to engage in the exchange of diverse goods and ideas.

The Scandinavians, driven by their desire for material wealth and prosperity, enthusiastically participated in trade activities. They offered commodities such as furs, walrus ivory, slaves, and timber to these more developed civilizations, in return for coveted treasures like silver, gold, luxury goods, and advancements in craftsmanship. The exchange of goods proved to be mutually beneficial for all parties involved, promoting economic growth and cultural exchange throughout the region.

However, these interactions with other civilizations had unintended consequences that would significantly reshape the Scandinavian world. The most transformative force that swept through these societies was the spread of Christianity. As pagan peoples, Scandinavians had long revered Norse gods such as Odin, Thor, and Freya, but the advent of Christianity challenged these traditional belief systems.

The process of Christian conversion in Scandinavia was not instantaneous; rather, it unfolded gradually and was met with fierce resistance. Despite the introduction of this new religious ideology, the old Norse gods continued to be openly worshipped in remote regions even into the Viking Age. This clash between different faiths heightened tensions within Scandinavian society – a tension that would have profound implications for the period.

Inherent in the clash between the old pagan religion and the new Christian faith were broader sociocultural dynamics. The collision of these belief systems symbolized the struggle between tradition and change, and the conflict between independence and conformity. These dynamics were instrumental in shaping the migrations and military ventures that characterized the Viking Age.

The clash of faiths fueled a deep sense of uncertainty and insecurity within Scandinavian communities. The transition from old gods to the teachings of Christianity involved not only changes in religious practices, but also in social norms, laws, and cultural traditions. This upheaval engendered a reactionary response among some Scandinavians, leading to resistance, rebellion, and a retreat into isolated regions that maintained the old ways.

In this atmosphere of religious turmoil, overarching societal tensions emerged. The desire to preserve and adhere to traditional values clashed with the pressures to conform to the new Christian ethos. This internal conflict fueled a complex interplay between the forces of tradition and change, individual freedom, and societal cohesion.

The tensions between tradition and change,

independence and conformity, were not limited to the realm of religion. They permeated all aspects of Scandinavian society, shaping its political, economic, and military landscape. These tensions, deeply rooted in the clash of faiths, motivated and influenced the Scandinavian migrations and military ventures that extended beyond their shores.

The Scandinavian societies, grappling with the disruption caused by their encounter with Christianity, sought to forge new paths and assert their independence in the wider world. They embarked on daring seafaring expeditions, known as Viking raids, that aimed to acquire wealth, resources, and prestige. These military ventures were driven, in part, by the desire to reclaim and anchor themselves in their ancestral traditions.

The Viking Age, characterized by seafaring raids, settlements, and trading expeditions, was a manifestation of the tension between the forces of tradition and change. The Scandinavian seafarers sought to establish their presence in new territories, forming their communities, and often assimilating within existing cultures. This nuanced blending of cultural traditions illustrates the intricate interplay between the desire for independence and the necessity for adaptation in a changing world.

Additionally, the Viking Age was not solely marked by military aggression. Scandinavians also engaged in extensive trade networks, acting as brokers between various civilizations. These economic endeavors further enriched Scandinavian societies and deepened their integration into the broader European landscape.

The Viking Age, therefore, represents a pivotal period in Scandinavian history, marked by the collision of faiths, the struggle between tradition and change, and the competing desires for independence and conformity. The dynamics at play during this era shed light on the motivations behind Scandinavian migrations and military ventures overseas, as well as their economic and cultural exchanges.

For the adventurous, restless spirits of Viking warriors and merchant traders, overseas exploration presented an opportunity for resources, riches, converts to their gods, or a chance to prove oneself in battle and gain honor, followers, and plunder otherwise unavailable in the tightly-knit, egalitarian Scandinavian communities. Their superb longships allowed navigation of major European rivers and coastlines with adaptive designs; wide-beamed vessels ideal for ocean voyages or more slender versions optimized for inland waterways. Vikings established settlements from Iceland and Greenland to the Shetland and Orkney Islands, the Faroe Islands, the coasts of Scotland, Ireland, England, the continent, and as far as North America many centuries before Columbus.

Major assaults initially came as surprise raids targeting lesser-defended monasteries, towns, and manors - hitting vulnerable economic, political, and religious centers with speed and ferocity before melting back into the seas or inland waterways. Monks were particular targets due to their valuable wares, and symbolism and because theological conflict erupted between pagan and Christian worldviews. Viking armies soon captured swaths of territory, establishing important governance and trade outposts - most prominently the Danelaw regions of northern/eastern England. Other groups fused with local populations, aided rulers, or formed new kingdoms as in Normandy, Sicily, and Kievan Rus' - spreading Scandinavian languages, customs, and DNA with broad and lasting genetic impacts across northern Europe and beyond.

While the plundering, slavery, and violence understandably generate grim associations with

Vikings, a balanced perspective acknowledges their profound cultural contributions as well. For peoples of the British Isles and Northern Europe, encounters with Vikings stimulated military, political, and economic reforms strengthening defenses. They revived long-distance trade routes and expanded geographical, botanical, and zoological knowledge. Technologies and skills were adopted/improved, from advanced shipbuilding techniques to new types of plows, swords, and ironworking. Runestones remained as a written language, while vocabulary, place names, and personal names of Norse origin pepper languages from Icelandic to English, Irish, Russian, and beyond. Most significantly, an enterprising spirit of exploration was stirred that would come to fruition with later European voyages of discovery.

At home in Scandinavia, Viking raids augmented regional power and prestige while trading profits enriched communities - spurring urbanization and sophisticated craftsmanship in jewelry, textiles, furniture, and more. Literary and artistic motifs absorbing Greek, Irish, Anglo-Saxon, and other continental influences enriched Scandinavian culture. Prosperity allowed monumental landmarks like garden cities, defensive fortifications, and important places of worship. Integration of migrant families broadened horizons. Yet the prevailing ethos stressed mastery, valor, protection of freedoms, and balance between ambition, community, and natural order. Though most famous as warriors, many Vikings also farmed, fished, or simply raised families - contributing to enduring

Nordic social cohesion and egalitarian democracy.

In the tumultuous era of the 10th century, a confluence of factors conspired to challenge agricultural productivity, leading to a deterioration of climactic conditions. This, combined with the diligent efforts of consolidated Christian monarchies and the relentless pressures of overpopulation, eventually led to the erosion of large-scale Viking raids. However, it is important to recognize that the indomitable spirit of the Vikings, forged through centuries of seafaring traditions, continued to thrive despite these circumstances.

While the heyday of Viking conquests may have waned, the Norsemen themselves continued to exert a profound influence on the course of history. They transitioned from their raider personas to become prominent figures in various domains, shaping the destiny of imperial Russia, serving as esteemed "Varangian" mercenaries for the Byzantine emperor, and assimilating as the "Northmen" in regions such as Normandy and northern England. This shift should not be seen as a defeat, but rather as a natural progression towards new stages of achievement through trade, diplomacy, and state-building. In doing so, the Scandinavians left an indelible mark and imbued their unique Scandinavian identity on the lands they encountered, stretching as far as Greenland and Sicily.

At the heart of this transformation, we witness an intriguing blend of consolidation and adaptation. While

Viking raids may have ebbed, the kings of Scandinavia seized the opportunity to consolidate their power and establish themselves as formidable rulers. Simultaneously, they astutely retained the ancient folkways that characterized their societies – participatory lawmaking and equality before the law. This amalgamation of old and new, of centralized governance and the preservation of traditional values, allows for the continued resilience and growth of Scandinavian society.

Trading ventures played a pivotal role in the transition of the Vikings from marauding warriors to esteemed merchants and diplomats. With their long-standing seafaring expertise, the Norsemen were uniquely positioned to capitalize on the emerging global networks of commerce. Establishing trade routes both within Europe and with distant lands, they utilized their navigational skills to connect cultures and foster economic prosperity. Through these enterprises, the Scandinavians not only expanded their influence but also facilitated cultural exchanges that enriched their society.

Furthermore, diplomacy became a vital tool in the Viking repertoire. They recognized that forging alliances and maintaining positive relations with foreign powers were essential for their continued success. This astute understanding propelled them to integrate themselves into the Byzantine Empire as "Varangian" mercenaries, a prestigious role that offered both economic opportunities and political advantages. This example serves as a testament to the Vikings' adaptability and their ability to seize opportunities, even in foreign lands.

While Vikings ventured far from their Scandinavian homelands, they remained strongly connected to their roots and continually left an indelible mark on their respective host societies. The Norman elite in France, descendants of Viking invaders who had previously settled in the region, retained a distinct Norse identity that significantly influenced cultural, linguistic, and political developments. Likewise, the Vikings who settled in northern England forged a lasting impact on the region, shaping its governance, economy, and even its language.

These far-reaching achievements were not, however, indicative of a complete abandonment of their heritage. Scandinavian societies experienced a unique form of political evolution, characterized by a delicate balance between centralized power and participatory lawmaking. While kings consolidated their authority, they did not relinquish the principles that made their societies cohesive and just. The institution of the "Thing" exemplified this commitment to egalitarian decision-making, with representatives from various social strata coming together to deliberate on matters of law and governance. This system, rooted in the folkways of the Vikings, ensured that the voices of all citizens were heard and contributed to the sense of solidarity and shared purpose that defined Scandinavian society.

In these tumultuous times, the Viking experience offers us invaluable guidance as we navigate the treacherous waters of our own lives. The Vikings, with their remarkable ability to adapt and flourish amidst adversity, provide us with a model of inspiration. They embody virtues such as courage, craftsmanship, cooperation, and a profound reverence for the awe-inspiring powers of nature. These qualities resonate deeply with us, urging us to explore the depths of our potential.

One of the most remarkable aspects of the Viking ethos is their unwavering spirit of innovation. They possessed a relentless pursuit of improvement and were not content with the status quo. Their independence of thought propelled them to defy the forces that sought to restrict their freedom and undermine their dignity. This indomitable spirit, combined with their refusal to bow down to oppressive forces, is something we can learn from and apply to our own lives.

While it is true that no era can be perfectly compared to another, certain values persist across time and transcend cultural boundaries. Protecting our autonomy through competence, fostering a sense of community, and accepting the responsibility to ensure a future that offers equal or greater opportunity than our own – these principles are worthy of upholding. By embracing uncertainty rather than succumbing to fear, and cultivating resilience, purpose, and meaningful connections with the world around us, we can discover our place in larger narratives and build foundations that future generations can build upon.

The Vikings demonstrate that this endeavor is not a mere fantasy. Even within the harshest of landscapes and eras, they found meaning and pursued betterment with unwavering tenacity. Their exploits remind us that we, too, possess the capacity to forge our paths and carve out a sense of purpose in our lives.

To fully grasp the depth and richness of the Viking experience, we must delve into their historical context. Their journey began in the Scandinavian region, a land of rugged beauty and harsh conditions. The unforgiving nature of their environment shaped them into hardy and resilient people. It was here, amidst the dramatic fjords, dense forests, and frigid winters, that the Vikings honed their survival skills and developed a deep respect for the power of nature.

Their interaction with the natural world gave rise to a profound reverence for its forces. They recognized their insignificance in the face of such magnificence, prompting a sense of humility that grounded their actions. This humility, coupled with an astute understanding of their surroundings, allowed them to work harmoniously with nature rather than attempting to dominate it. Their craftsmanship, whether it be shipbuilding, weaponry, or intricate artwork, was a testament to their ability to harness the resources at their disposal and create beauty from the raw materials of their environment.

The Vikings were not simply conquerors and raiders; they were also skilled traders and explorers. Their ships, the iconic longboats, became symbols of their seafaring prowess and their insatiable thirst for discovery. With these vessels, they ventured into uncharted waters, bravely facing the unknown and expanding their horizons. Their expeditions took them to far-flung lands, forging connections with diverse cultures and leaving a lasting impact on the world.

Yet, what truly sets the Viking experience apart is their commitment to the ideals of autonomy and freedom. They valiantly defended their independence, refusing to submit to forces that sought to diminish their dignity. To the Vikings, freedom was not a mere abstract concept – it was a fundamental aspect of their identity. They fiercely protected their autonomy through their competence in various domains, be it combat, trade, or craftsmanship.

It is this commitment to autonomy that resonates deeply with the modern individual. In our present age, where societal structures often seem to encroach upon our liberty, the Viking ethos reminds us of the importance of personal agency. By cultivating competence in our chosen pursuits – whether it be in our careers, relationships, or personal development – we can safeguard our autonomy and resist the forces that seek to control us.

However, the Vikings understood that true autonomy is

not isolating oneself from society. They relied on cooperation and community to fortify their independence. They recognized that collective strength was essential for survival and progress. The bonds they formed within their communities, built on trust, mutual support, and shared values, allowed them to weather storms and thrive in the face of adversity.

This interconnectedness is a lesson we can integrate into our own lives. In a world where individualism often takes center stage, fostering meaningful connections with others can provide us with a sense of belonging and purpose. By engaging in collaborative endeavors, we can harness the power of collective action and create a better future for ourselves and those who will come after us.

As we navigate the challenges of our era, we must not lose sight of the importance of leaving a meaningful legacy for future generations. The Vikings understood this responsibility, striving to ensure that their successors would inherit opportunities and resources comparable to their own. They had a profound reverence for the notion of intergenerational equity and recognized the profound impact their actions would have on those who would follow in their footsteps.

In an age marked by environmental degradation, social inequality, and countless other pressing issues, we are called upon to embrace this responsibility. By considering the long-term consequences of our actions and making sustainable choices, we can ensure that future generations inherit a world that offers them the same – if not greater – opportunities and resources than we currently enjoy.

Embracing the Viking experience goes beyond mere historical curiosity. It urges us to explore our potential and strive for excellence in all aspects of our lives. Their story teaches us that even within the most challenging landscapes and eras, meaning and betterment are within our grasp. By channeling the Viking spirit of innovation, independence of thought, and reverence for the natural world, we can forge our paths and construct foundations that future generations can build upon.

The Viking Age demonstrated how character strengths

like courage, perseverance, and innovativeness can empower people to surmount immense challenges and shape history. While known for their daring raids, Vikings also spread cultural currents with enduring impacts through exploration, trade, and settlement across wide spheres. At home in Scandinavia, they helped establish societal templates balancing communal cohesion and individual liberties that proved robust for many generations. Their saga contains lessons still applicable for forging purpose and meaning amid life's unpredictability. By cultivating fortitude of spirit, investing in families and communities, passing on responsibility for futurity, and grasping opportunities that change brings – as Vikings did so well - individuals and peoples may continue growing in positive directions even within tumultuous times. Their epic adventure epitomizes humanity at its finest.

Viking Age in Sweden

Deep in the Norse myths and legends lies prototypical wisdom about the relationship between civilization and the wilderness it wrestles from. When gods like Odin abandoned primordial order to bring language, culture, and agricultural progress to Scandinavia's domains, they knew change would not come without conflict and necessary sacrifice. No place embodied this interplay of constraints and potentials quite like Sweden during the dynamic Viking Age - where hardy peoples balanced village and forest, raid and trade, force and diplomacy to eventually forge a unified kingdom from their island-strewn landscape. Their saga rewards reflection, as disruption always tests both social bonds and individual character.

Sweden's geographically remote location in the northern reaches of Europe presented both challenges and opportunities for its early inhabitants. The intricate coastline, adorned with deep fjords and numerous islands, bays, and inlets, bestowed the perfect conditions for the Viking longships to navigate and establish prosperous coastal communities. These seafaring settlements relied on their maritime skills, woodcraft, animal husbandry, and the extraction of iron from bogs to sustain their way of life.

However, venturing inland revealed an entirely different terrain. Thick taiga forests and untamed highlands dominated the interior regions of Sweden, making it formidable for agricultural endeavors. The short growing seasons imposed further limitations on farming, forcing communities to adapt their strategies for survival. To flourish amidst these environmental constraints, the coastal communities had to exploit the full potential of their unique resources and develop specialized skills.

The absence of a centralized authority played a significant role in shaping the social and political landscape of early Sweden. Instead of unified governance, the region witnessed the emergence of several petty kingdoms, each defined by kin-based loyalties, distinct local dialects, and folk customs. This decentralized system created a sense of regionalism, with the communities of Sweden's various regions maintaining their own distinct identities and ways of life.

In the ever-changing tapestry of Sweden's early history, the coastal communities stood out as bastions of life and progress. With their mastery of the seas, they connected the landlocked interior with the rest of Scandinavia and beyond. The Viking longships not only facilitated trade but also opened up avenues for exploration and conquest, fostering a rich exchange of cultures, and ideas, and ultimately, the expansion of Sweden's influence.

The coastal communities' reliance on maritime skills became a defining characteristic of their identity. Skillful navigation, expert shipbuilding, and fishing prowess were crucial for their survival and prosperity. It was in the crucible of the sea that they honed their aptitude for exploration, their fearlessness in the face of the unknown, and their keen sense of adventure.

Woodcraft, too, played a vital role in the coastal communities' way of life. The dense forests that covered much of the land provided not only shelter but also a bountiful source of raw materials. The skillful manipulation of wood allowed the communities to construct sturdy ships, durable homes, and other essential tools for their daily existence. Through generations of expertise and innovation, the art of woodcraft became ingrained within their cultural fabric and passed down from one generation to the next.

Animal husbandry, with its inherent connection to the land, offered yet another avenue for sustenance and economic stability. The coastal communities, well aware of the limitations imposed by their harsh environment, adapted their strategies accordingly. By domesticating and raising livestock, they could supplement their diets with meat, milk, and other animal byproducts, ensuring a more reliable food source in the face of unpredictable harvests and limited agricultural potential.

However, one must not overlook the significance of Sweden's bogs in these early settlements. Hidden within the marshy landscape lay vast deposits of iron, a precious resource that would shape the destiny of both the coastal and inland communities alike. Extracting iron from these bogs required intricate knowledge and skilled craftsmanship. Through a meticulous process of burning, heating, and smelting, the settlers transformed the raw materials into essential tools and weapons, vital for their survival and progress. This mastery of iron extraction from the bogs became an integral part of their identity and contributed significantly to their prosperity and influence.

This decentralized landscape, characterized by petty kingdoms and regionalism, had its unique advantages and disadvantages. On one hand, it allowed for a deep sense of community and loyalty amongst its inhabitants. The kin-based loyalties that defined these petty kingdoms ensured a strong social fabric, where each member felt a sense of belonging and protection. Local dialects and folk customs also thrived within these smaller communities, fostering a strong cultural identity that was intimately intertwined with the land and its traditions.

On the other hand, this decentralized authority structure presented challenges when it came to governance and cohesion. The absence of a central power meant that conflicts between petty kingdoms were not uncommon. Disputes over resources, territory, or even simply matters of honor could escalate into full-fledged conflicts, threatening the stability and progress of the region as a whole. These regional rivalries, fueled by familial and kin-based alliances, often perpetuated cycles of violence that hindered the development of a unified Swedish identity.

The multifaceted nature of Sweden's early history paints a vivid picture of a land that bore witness to both the hardships of isolation and the opportunities for growth offered by its unique geography. The coastal communities, with their mastery of the sea, woodcraft, animal husbandry, and bog-based iron extraction, persevered in the face of adversity and thrived. Their close-knit societies, defined by kin-based loyalties and local customs, exemplified the power of regionalism and contributed to the diverse tapestry of Sweden's past.

As we contemplate the foundations upon which nations are built, it becomes evident that Sweden's early history holds valuable lessons. The union of communal expertise, environmental adaptability, and regional cohesion, while simultaneously embracing the exploratory spirit, helped forge a resilient society capable of facing any challenge. The legacy left by the coastal communities and their counterparts in the interior weaves a narrative of innovation, resilience, and an unwavering commitment to survival.

Sweden's position as a remote northern nation may have initially posed obstacles, but it also birthed opportunities. It is in the unique blend of challenges and advantages that we find the true essence of Sweden's early history—a testament to the triumph of human ingenuity in the face of adversity. Today, as we navigate our uncharted waters, we can draw inspiration from the coastal communities of Sweden, their mastery of the seas, and their unwavering spirit to overcome any obstacle on the path to progress.

This dispersed geography necessitated cooperation but also bred an independent spirit. Warriors formed the nucleus of society, and military skill, cunning strategy, or daring raids could elevate minor Jarls to kings of amalgamated territories. Success on the battlefield brought wealth, prestige, and followers to warlords - yet daily sustenance required a balance between ambition, subsistence duties, and maintaining ties between communities. Poetry remembers Odin-following kings like Egil Skallagrimsson who fused Viking ferocity with state-building intellect when interests aligned.

Contact and conflict with more developed realms eventually presented Swedes opportunity to enrich their existence through exposure and enterprise abroad. Between the 8th to 11th centuries, Swedish Vikings launched hit-and-run attacks and longer-term conquests from the British Isles and Frankish kingdoms to Baltic and eastern European river trade routes. Major Swedish dynasty lines like the legendary House of Munsö grew wealthy and influential through a blend of raiding, trading, and colonizing endeavors. Towns like Sigtuna and Birka served as communications hubs where merchants from throughout the Nordic world and beyond mingled.

Such exposure stirred emulation of more advanced societies like the Franks while spreading Swedish cultural currents in turn. Urbanization accompanied the rise of craft and merchant classes dealing in prized exports like fur, wax, honey, slaves, lumber, and iron. Contacts with Christianity constituted another arena of tension between conservatism and modernity - intensifying as Swedish rulers converted and centralized power under Göta King Olof Skötkonung and his successors. Gradually, the integration and assimilation of foreign populations enlarged Sweden's map and horizons beyond its original borders and diversified the gene pool.

Evidence of Swedish settlements stretches from the Russian river trade networks and Scandinavian outposts like Garðaríki to the coasts of England and Normandy, where locals came to be known as the "Northmen." The Danelaw region of eastern England fell under Scandinavian control for over a century. More distant voyages may have reached Greenland, Iceland the Faroe Islands, and even North America leading some to speculate Norse discovery of the New World predated by centuries later European expeditions. Wherever Swedes went, they blended pragmatism and assertiveness, crafting alliances or imposing authority as strategic circumstances required.

In the vast expanse of history, the legacy of the Swedish Vikings stands as a testament to their sheer impact on both domestic and international fronts. These fervent seafarers not only sailed across treacherous waters but also brought with them a wealth of cultural, economic, and linguistic treasures, forever altering the course of history.

Trade, for instance, played a pivotal role in the cultural diffusion catalyzed by the Vikings. With the rise of Gotland as a central marketplace, an unprecedented acceleration in the exchange of goods, ideas, and traditions ensued. This bustling trading hub served as a meeting point for diverse cultures and facilitated the spread of knowledge, technologies, and artistic creations. The echoes of this vibrant cultural exchange can still be witnessed today, as the toponyms scattered throughout lands influenced by the Vikings bear witness to the new farming techniques, tools, and place name structures implanted by settlers of yore.

In addition to their invaluable contributions to the realm of commerce, the military might of the Vikings left an indelible mark on the nations they encountered during their raids and conquests. In regions such as England and Ireland, the Vikings' relentless invasions stimulated a need for defensive fortifications and often led to the political reunification of fragmented territories. These defensive structures not only stood as a tangible manifestation of the Vikings' military domination but also played a crucial role in shaping the political landscape of the invaded regions. The echoes of the Vikings' martial prowess reverberated throughout history, shaping the destinies of kingdoms and forging alliances that endure to this day.

No exploration of the impacts of the Vikings would be complete without considering their linguistic legacy. From the rural idioms of the Dales to the very word for "war" in the Russian language, the Vikings' linguistic imprint has pervaded countless cultures and tongues. Their influence can be discerned in the numerous loanwords and expressions that have weaved themselves into the fabric of various languages. One cannot but marvel at the far-reaching consequences of Viking linguistic influence, spanning both time and space, forever altering the way we communicate and conceptualize our world.

To fully grasp the implications of Swedish Viking activity, it becomes imperative to delve further into their rich tapestry of influence, extending beyond the borders of their homeland. The Vikings, through their extensive trade networks, engulfed the seas and penetrated foreign lands, leaving an enduring legacy in their wake. The vibrant economic exchanges took place not only through Gotland but also via the sprawling network of Norse settlements and trading posts that stretched from Greenland to the Byzantine Empire.

The impact of this maritime connectivity cannot be overstated, as it heralded a new era of cultural diffusion unrivaled in its breadth and depth. The Swedes, with their insatiable curiosity and thirst for exploration, became purveyors of knowledge, carrying with them not only exotic goods but also a plethora of ideas and innovations. Through these interactions, Sweden became a conduit for the exchange of technologies, enabling the dissemination of new farming techniques and tools that forever altered the agricultural practices of the lands under their sway.

However, it is not solely in the realm of agriculture that the Vikings' imprint can be discerned. The linguistic landscape of the territories they traversed bears the indomitable mark of their presence. From the British Isles to the vast reaches of Russia, the echoes of Viking tongues still resound in countless idioms, expressions, and linguistic borrowings. Through this linguistic exchange, the Vikings not only communicated but also permeated the very fabric of the societies they encountered, leaving an enduring imprint on their languages and shaping regional dialects in ways that are still evident today.

Yet, it is not only through peaceful trade and linguistic exchanges that the Vikings left their mark. The bane of many coastal communities, their raids were not only a testament to their prowess as seafarers but also a force that spurred monumental changes in the regions they targeted. The relentless invasions of England and

Ireland, for instance, left an indelible impact on the lands and peoples they encountered. The Vikings' military domination often led to the establishment of defensive fortifications, driving the conquered territories to fortify themselves against future incursions.

These fortifications became not only symbols of defense but also centers of power and political reunification. The Vikings unwittingly served as catalysts, fueling the consolidation of fragmented regions and heralding the emergence of larger political entities. In the case of England, the Danish conquerors eventually assimilated into the local population, leading to the establishment of the Danelaw and reshaping the power dynamics of the land. Indeed, the

Vikings' invasions and subsequent presence left an ineffaceable fingerprint on the political landscape of foreign lands, forever altering the course of history.

Thus, the far-reaching impacts of Swedish Viking activity are undeniable, leaving an indomitable legacy that transcends time and space. Their thirst for trade accelerated cultural diffusion, creating vibrant marketplaces that brought together diverse cultures and fueled the exchange of goods, ideas, and technologies. The farming techniques, tools, and place names they implanted continue to live on today, illuminating the path of their enduring influence. The Vikings' military domination, though wrought with strife, fostered the construction of defensive fortifications and reshaped political entities, leaving lasting imprints on the lands they invaded. And perhaps most remarkably, the linguistic legacy of the Vikings resonates across multiple languages, forever etching their presence in the very words we speak and the concepts we convey. The Swedish Vikings, with their insatiable curiosity and audacity, forever altered the tapestry of history, leaving an awe-inspiring testament to the power and enduring impact of human endeavor.

The sagas of North American Vinland shed light upon the origins of the spirit that would come to be so integral to the modern Swedish national identity - the pioneering and adventurous nature of the frontiersmen. Even in those early times, we can see the seeds of this spirit taking root. However, as is often the case, kingdoms will inevitably face the consequences of their actions, and the return of these warriors to their homelands began to strain the egalitarian values of their communal societies.

By the waning years of the Viking Age, specifically around 1050 AD, a significant shift was occurring. Monarchs such as Saint Olav Haraldsson emerged, their primary focus being the propagation of Christianity throughout the land. These centralized leaders, while instrumental in the process of Christianization, began imposing taxes upon the prosperous agriculturists and merchants to sustain their expanding power. The integration of these Christian values, coupled with the growing influence of these monarchs, had profound effects on the social fabric of the time.

Simultaneously, as the power of the centralized monarchs grew, the influence of the chieftains began to wane. These chieftains, who had once ruled as independent leaders in their own right, gradually consolidated their power and assumed the titles of jarls. This consolidation can be seen as an attempt to maintain their status and authority amidst the changing landscape of Viking society.

The implications of these transformations were far-reaching. The once-strong sense of communal spirit and egalitarian values that had characterized the Viking society began to erode under the weight of these societal changes. No longer were individuals bound by the shared pursuit of a common goal, but rather, they were subjected to the whims and demands of these increasingly powerful jarls.

The consequences of these developments also impacted the relationships between these jarls and the common people. While the jarls held onto their positions of privilege and authority, the burden of increased taxes and obligations fell upon the agricultural and merchant classes.

Furthermore, the influence of Christianity introduced a new set of values and beliefs that further undermined the communal fabric of Viking society. The Christian faith preached the virtues of humility, submission, and obedience to a higher power. These teachings ran counter to the fiercely independent and self-reliant nature that had defined the Viking way of life. As Christianity took hold, the individualistic spirit of the Vikings began to give way to a more hierarchical and obedient mindset.

In the long term, Sweden underwent a transformative transition out of its raiding phase, ultimately strengthening its unity and cohesion. This transition laid the foundation for the country's future imperial greatness, establishing it as a model agricultural economy and expanding its frontiers. The emergence of major seafaring and merchant families, most notably the influential Folkungs, played a pivotal role in assimilating or aiding ecclesiastical rulers, further solidifying Sweden's steady ascent.

Moreover, the utilization of peatlands as an abundant source of fuel propelled the success of charcoal-fed blast furnaces, leading to the production of high-quality iron exports. This, in turn, bolstered Sweden's economic prowess, establishing the nation as a significant player in the international trade arena. The efficient utilization of resources and the development of thriving industries set the stage for Sweden's future economic growth and prosperity.

Sociopolitical stability was of utmost importance during this transformative period, and Sweden managed to strike a delicate balance between a hierarchical nobility and an independent bonder class. The establishment of this sturdy framework allowed for the effective distribution of authority and power, while simultaneously permitting democratic local governance. This delicate equilibrium provided the necessary stability that endured for generations, enabling Sweden to navigate through the complexities of governance with resilience and sagacity.

Despite the waning influence of pagan beliefs during this era, a proud and distinctive Swedish cultural identity continued to shine through various avenues. Folk traditions, runic inscriptions, and artistic motifs served as powerful mediums through which the echoes of their Viking heritage resounded. These cultural practices not only preserved Sweden's historical roots but also fostered a sense of national belonging and pride, further solidifying the collective identity of the Swedish people.

Sweden's transition out of its raiding phase and the subsequent developments that followed exemplify the nation's remarkable ability to adapt, evolve, and thrive. The agricultural revolution, expansive frontiers, and industrious enterprises propelled Sweden onto the path of greatness. The integration of influential seafaring and merchant families, such as the esteemed Folkungs, into the fabric of governance ensured continuity and stability. Additionally, the utilization of natural resources, particularly the peatlands serving as an abundant source of fuel for the blast furnaces, fueled the economic growth and success that marked this transformative era.

Moreover, the establishment of a robust social

framework, characterized by a hierarchical nobility and an independent bonder class, struck a delicate balance between authority and democratic local governance. This unique system provided stability and resilience, allowing Sweden to navigate through the complexities of governance and administration with remarkable efficacy.

While the influence of pagan beliefs diminished, Swedish cultural identity remained steadfast and vibrant. Through vibrant folk traditions, captivating runic inscriptions, and evocative artistic motifs, the echoes of the Viking heritage were kept alive. These cultural practices not only served as a testament to Sweden's rich history but also fostered a profound sense of national pride and belonging. The cultural continuity nurtured during this period became an integral part of Sweden's collective identity, shaping the nation as it continued to embrace its future endeavors.

As Sweden emerged stronger and more cohesive from its raiding phase, it etched its name onto the annals of history, becoming a model for other nations to follow. The nation's agricultural prowess, which laid the groundwork for future imperial greatness, was complemented by the expansion of its frontiers. Sweden's ability to harness the potential of its natural resources, such as the peatlands fueling the booming iron industry, showcased its economic might and placed it prominently on the global stage.

In the realms of governance and social structure, Sweden distinguished itself with a well-balanced system, combining the authority of a hierarchical nobility with the democratic principles of local governance. This delicate equilibrium ensured that power was distributed effectively and that the needs of the people were met. The stability resulting from this system throughout generations solidified Sweden's reputation as a beacon of governance and a haven of societal cohesion.

The preservation of cultural identity became a crucial characteristic of the Swedish nation during this transformative period. While paganism gradually receded into the background, the proud Swedish heritage endured through various cultural expressions.

From lively folk traditions and meticulously carved runic inscriptions to the mesmerizing artistic motifs that adorned everyday life, Sweden celebrated its Viking past. This cultural continuity not only preserved the nation's historical roots but also served as a source of inspiration and shared pride for Swedes across generations.

Sweden's transition out of its raiding phase marked the beginning of a new era defined by economic prosperity, sociopolitical stability, and cultural cohesiveness. The nation's agricultural developments, expansive frontiers, and industrial enterprises laid the foundation for its imperial greatness. Influential seafaring families, exemplified by the Folkungs, played a central role in governance, strengthening the bond between ecclesiastical rulers and the ruling elite. The abundant peatlands fueled the blast furnaces, propelling Sweden's iron industry to unprecedented heights. The establishment of a balanced sociopolitical framework harmonized authority and democratic local governance, fostering stability that would persist for generations.

Although pagan beliefs gradually faded, Swedish cultural identity continued to resonate through folk traditions, runic inscriptions, and artistic motifs, echoing the vibrant heritage of the Vikings. Through their remarkable adaptability, resilience, and a strong sense of national pride, the Swedish people emerged from this transformative period stronger, more cohesive, and poised to shape their destiny as a remarkable nation in the vast tapestry of history.

The Viking Age allowed enterprising Swedes to spread wings outward and draw sustenance home in kind. Their formidable longships and fearsome reputation belied pragmatic goals of acquiring resources, new lands, and lucrative trade routes interweaving Scandinavia with European and Eurasian networks. Though raids shook imperiled realms, Swedish migrants and merchants also transmitted infrastructure, technologies, administrative practices, and linguistic influences amid turbulent times of transition. Most importantly, encounters abroad honed independence and ingenuity that served Swedes well as they solidified the foundations of national identity and physical territory during later state-building eras.

Vigorous, industrious, and family-oriented - qualities so core to modern Swedish culture find their roots in the hardy soil tilled first by those ingenious island folk of the north.

Vikings' Legacy in Swedish Culture

A people's collective ancestry forms the bedrock of who they become - for better and worse - across generations. In 2010, a genetic study revealed over 80% of men living in Sweden carry ancestral lineages tracing back to stone-age Scandinavian farmers. Yet it was during another transformative era, the turbulent

Viking Age of raids, exploration, and state-building between 793-1066 CE, that Sweden's national character truly began taking distinctive shape. Since then, the resilient, independent, and innovative spirit that empowered mighty Norse warriors and seafaring merchants to shape destinies from Newfoundland to Normandy persists in Swedish society today, visible across customs, traditions, and cultural touchpoints large and small.

As one strolls along the streets of any Swedish town, it is impossible to ignore the echoes of a rich and storied past that seem to emanate from every nook and cranny. The centuries-old buildings and monuments that line these streets carry with them the indelible imprint of the mighty Vikings, those fierce seafaring warriors who once ruled these lands. If one takes the time to truly immerse oneself in the surroundings, even the most inconspicuous elements can offer profound insights into the Viking-era roots that lie buried beneath the surface.

Take, for instance, the remarkable stave churches that can be found sprinkled across the Swedish landscape. These architectural relics, with their intricate woodwork and unmistakable Nordic charm, provide us with a tangible link to a bygone era. They stand as a testament to the faith of our ancestors, who sought solace in these hallowed halls and sought to solidify their connection to the divine. The stave churches, adorned with their ornate carvings and symbols, not only served as places of worship but also embodied a distinct architectural style that was uniquely Viking, blending elements of paganism and Christianity.

And then there are the runic inscriptions that adorn village stones and hidden corners, silently whispering tales of a time long past. These ancient writings, etched with care and precision, tell stories of conquest, love, and reverence for the gods. They remind us that the Vikings were not just fearless warriors but also a people with a profound appreciation for the written word, and for the power it had to immortalize their deeds and ensure their legacy.

But it is not just in these tangible remnants of the past that we can find traces of our Viking ancestors. Even in the very names of the places that dot our landscape, the layers of history are laid bare for those with a discerning eye. Rivers like the Göta Älv, a majestic waterway that weaves its way through the heart of the country, offer us a glimpse into the Gothic-era travel routes that our forefathers once trod. These vital arteries of transportation and trade not only connected inland communities but also maintained the intricate web of tribal confederations that defined the social fabric of the time. They were the lifeblood of our ancestors' civilization, ensuring their survival and prosperity.

And then there is the name by which we refer to ourselves, the very identity that unites us as a people - Svear, or "Swedes." This word, seemingly simple at first glance, carries within it a profound connection to our origins. It is a name that harkens back to the patrimonial kingdom of Svealand, the very heartland from which our great nation emerged. Svealand, centered on the modern regions of Uppland and Södermanland, served as the epicenter of power and authority, the central pillar around which our ancestral tribes were united. To be a Svear was to be part of a lineage, to belong and be cherished, to feel the weight of responsibility and heritage on one's shoulders. It is this deep-rooted connection to our past that continues to shape our present and guide our future.

Walking through the streets of any Swedish town is not simply a journey through time; it is an exploration of the essence of what it means to be Swedish. The buildings and monuments that surround us serve as physical reminders of the sacrifices and triumphs of our Viking ancestors. The stave churches stand as enduring testaments to their religious fervor, while the runic inscriptions etched in stone bear witness to their creativity and passion for storytelling. The very names of our towns and rivers evoke a sense of pride and belonging, a recognition that we are part of something greater than ourselves.

But beyond merely appreciating the relics of the past, we must also strive to learn from them. The Viking era was a time of exploration, innovation, and resilience. Our ancestors ventured far and wide, leaving their mark on distant lands and forging new paths of trade and discovery. They were not content to remain within the confines of their homeland; they were driven by an insatiable curiosity and an unquenchable thirst for knowledge. It is this spirit of exploration and determination that we must embrace if we are to honor the legacy of those who came before us.

In the centuries since the Vikings walked these lands, Sweden has evolved and transformed. We have faced countless challenges and overcome numerous obstacles, but throughout it all, we have remained anchored in our past. The rich tapestry of history that weaves its way through every fiber of our being serves as a constant reminder of who we are and what we are capable of. It is a reminder that, like our Viking ancestors, we have the strength and resilience to overcome any adversity that comes our way.

The core cultural orientations that we observe today are deeply rooted in the Nordic past. The Nordic region, comprising countries such as Sweden, Norway, Denmark, Finland, and Iceland, has forged a unique identity through millennia of history. Within this cultural tapestry, we find echoes of the once-mighty Vikings and their way of life.

One fundamental aspect of Nordic culture that reverberates throughout their political traditions is the commitment to egalitarianism and consensus. These values, which prioritize cooperation over authoritarianism, can be traced back to the loosely governed clans and things (assemblies) that the Vikings formed to represent their coastal communities. In these societies, decision-making was often achieved through discussion and negotiation, to ensure that everyone had a voice. This democratic spirit, born out of necessity in the face of harsh and unforgiving environments, has been interwoven into the fabric of Nordic societies to this day.

Another key aspect of Nordic culture that aligns with their Viking ancestry is the fierce valuing of freedom, self-sufficiency, and a strong work ethic. This ethos can be understood within the context of the ancestral struggles against nature in the northern lands. The Nordic people have long had to contend with harsh climates, where survival depended on one's ability to fend for themselves. Enduring the relentless battles against the elements instilled in them a deep appreciation for personal autonomy and self-reliance.

This mindset, deeply intertwined with their cultural DNA, continues to be upheld and celebrated as a virtue in Nordic societies.

When examining the Nordic region's cultural landscape, one cannot ignore the prevalence of stoicism, understatement, and practicality. These qualities have come to define the Nordic mentality and can be seen as reflections of the survival imperatives that the people have long faced. Inhabiting punishing climes for generations has demanded a certain level of resilience and emotional restraint. Stoicism, in particular, has allowed the Nordic people to weather the storms of life without succumbing to despair. By embracing understatement and practicality, they have adapted themselves to endure and thrive in challenging circumstances.

Furthermore, these traits are deeply rooted in the dignity of honest labor, craftsmanship, and familial bonds. The concept of honor and pride in one's work is an integral part of the Nordic identity, resonating from a time when manual labor and craftsmanship were essential for survival and prosperity. Scandinavian societies have long placed a premium on the skills and integrity required to produce high-quality products and services. This focus on craftsmanship and labor is not only a source of personal pride but also reinforces the strong family bonds that characterize Nordic society, where each member has a crucial part to play in ensuring collective well-being.

Within the rich tapestry of Nordic culture, we also encounter Sweden's famous sense of lagom. Lagom, a uniquely Swedish term, encapsulates the concept of balance, participation, and collective prospering within natural limits. This notion of finding the appropriate measure, neither too much nor too little, exemplifies the wisdom inherited from the Viking ancestors. The Vikings, known for their seafaring ventures, understood all too well the importance of finding the middle path in life. They navigated treacherous seas, always seeking to strike a delicate equilibrium between ambition and caution. This holistic approach, grounded in the understanding of natural limits, continues to shape the Swedish psyche, fostering a society that strives for harmony and sustainable prosperity.

In the vast tapestry of human history, certain threads remain steadfast, weaving together the past with the present. As we venture into the 21st century, it is remarkable to witness how many traditional folkways and festivals persist, bearing within them the echoes of pre-Christian customs. These age-old rituals, handed down through generations, possess a profound resonance, as they seamlessly intermingle with later Christian meanings. One such celebration that captures this entwining of traditions is the enchanting Midsommar festival, a captivating event that harks back to ancient pagan rites while embracing elements of Christian symbolism.

Step back in time to an era when the rhythms of life were intricately intertwined with the cycle of the seasons, and the spiritual connection between nature and mankind was palpable. The summer solstice, heralding the longest day of the year and the pinnacle of vitality in the natural world, bore immense significance for our ancestors. In their unwavering pursuit of agricultural fertility and the eternal struggle against malevolent forces, communities would gather in fields and groves for the sacred Midsommar rites.

Picture, if you will, the vivid landscapes adorned with flickering bonfires, maypoles bedecked with ribbons, and garlands of vibrant wildflowers. These picturesque scenes, redolent with the scent of nature's bounty, mirrored the solemn homage paid by our forebears to the sun god Baldur. Bathed in the warm glow of the bonfires, communities would engage in a delicate dance of appeasing the divine forces that governed the fertility of their crops. By making offerings to Baldur, beseeching his favor and protection, they sought to ensure the prosperity of their fields and ward off the lurking specter of evil.

In the dance of history, the pagan traditions of Midsommar were not lost but instead fused with the encroaching tendrils of Christian beliefs. As the early Christian conversion swept through Europe, the Church, out of a pragmatic necessity, sought to integrate pre-existing customs into their practices to facilitate a smoother transition. Thus, the celebration of Midsommar became interwoven with the commemoration of the birth of St. John the Baptist, a significant figure in Christian tradition. The radiant bonfires, reminiscent of the ancient sacred flames, now symbolized the illumination brought by John the Baptist, heralding the arrival of Christ as the light of the world.

Emerging from the depths of history, let us now turn our gaze towards the frost-kissed landscapes of winter, where the ever-lengthening nights give way to the return of the sun's life-giving rays. Santa Lucia's procession and the treasured Yule log tradition both anchor themselves in the pre-Christian observances of the winter solstice. In those darkest days of the year, when fear and uncertainty gripped the hearts of our ancestors, rituals were enacted to rejoice in the anticipation of the sun's triumphant journey back to its former strength.

The ethereal beauty of Santa Lucia's procession shimmers through the centuries, as a young woman adorned with a wreath of candles adorns the crown of her head, illuminating the night with her grace. This powerful symbol of light prevailing over darkness crystallizes the yearning of generations past, desperately seeking the return of longer days and the subsequent revival of nature's fecundity. In Scandinavian cultures, Lucia is a cherished cultural figure, embodying hope and resilience during the bleak winter season—a testament to the enduring influence of pre-Christian solstice traditions that refuse to be extinguished.

Akin to a roaring hearth in the great hall of history, the

Yule log tradition blazes across time, illuminating the customs of our ancestors. Deeply rooted in the observances of the winter solstice, when bonfires were kindled in hearths to beckon the sun's return, the Yule log became a central component of winter festivities. With reverential care, families would select a large log, meticulously choosing one that embodied strength and warmth. This log, symbolizing the life force within the hearth, would then be ceremoniously ignited, its flames evoking the promise of longer days to come. As the Yule log slowly burnt, its smoky tendrils whispering sacred secrets into the air, families would gather, exchanging stories and partaking in conviviality, defying the harsh winter nights with love and laughter.

Indeed, through the ages, these seemingly disparate

folkways and festivals effortlessly intertwine with the tapestry of human existence, their vibrant threads coloring the fabric of our collective identity. Traditional customs celebrating the solstices, be it the summer's zenith or winter's nadir, occupy a special place in our hearts, forging a connection between our ancestors and ourselves. As we venture forth into this modern epoch, it is a testament to the enduring human spirit that we preserve and perpetuate these age-old rituals, breathing life into the ancient echoes of our pre-Christian heritage.

Woven within the fabric of Swedish culture lies a tapestry of living poetry and stories that have been passed down since Viking times. These tales, communicated through ancient runes, are the very essence of our cultural heritage, serving as both cautionary lessons and exemplars of virtue. They stand as a bulwark against forgetfulness and moral decay, ensuring that the spirit of honor and integrity endures across the ages.

The epic poems of the Poetic Edda and Prose Edda, along with regional ballads and folktales, paint a vivid picture of the heroics and sagas that have shaped our identity as Swedes. These narratives, steeped in mythological imagery, resonate with a timeless impact that speaks to the strengths and frailties of the Swedish people. Through the characters of Odin, Thor, Loki, and Freyja, we find archetypal representations of the human experience.

Loki, with his cunning trickery and deceptions, serves as a stark reminder of the corruption that can lurk within each of us. His presence in these tales is a testament to the reality of human nature, demonstrating that even the noblest individuals may have hidden flaws. In contrast, Odin's sacrifice of an eye for divine inspiration serves as a powerful call to embark on a quest for deeper meaning. This sacrifice exemplifies the idea that true enlightenment and growth often come at a great cost, requiring us to embrace uncertainty, take risks, and make sacrifices for the greater good.

It is these mythic narratives that fuel our national pride, connecting modern Swedes to the brave explorers, traders, and warrior-poets who expanded the boundaries of our world. The tales of Ragnar

Lodbrok's legendary raids, Ivar the Boneless and his Great Heathen Army carving the Danelaw, and Leif Eriksson setting foot on North American shores long before Columbus evoke a deep sense of awe and admiration. These stories remind us of the qualities that allowed our ancestors to thrive – perseverance, courage, and adaptability.

Through their adventures, our ancestors spread not only Swedish culture but also our genetic lineages across hemispheres. This legacy of exploration and expansion is a testament to the indomitable spirit that has driven the Swedish people throughout history. We can take pride in knowing that our ancestors played a crucial role in shaping the world as we know it today.

The tales of these bold men and women serve as a constant reminder that we, too, have the potential to achieve greatness. Their achievements were not borne out of luck or happenstance but rather through their unwavering commitment to their ideals and their willingness to embrace challenges head-on. By embracing the lessons embedded within these stories, we can tap into the wellspring of strength and resilience that lies within each of us.

The same spirited independence lives on in Swedish customs. Take the continued popularity of folk music and dance styles like polska and schottis whose lively two-steps and swirling figures stem from ancient pastoral rhythms. Or consider how Swedes still give voice to that elemental Viking spirit come mid-winter yuletide gatherings, cozying by firesides with hearty glögg wine, pickled herring, ham, rye bread, and stories - simple pleasures sustainably connecting to Nordic roots in ways globalized elsewhere. People sense weaving between past grandeur and present-day practicalities nurtures societal well-being across the lifespan.

This enduring cultural bond with the Viking era serves as a powerful psychological anchor for Sweden, granting its people a source of collective pride and solace amidst the uncertainties of the modern world. As globalization sweeps across the globe, eroding age-old traditions and values, the indomitable spirit that ignited in Scandinavia's northern lands serves as a steadfast bulwark against the tides of change. By venerating the triumphs and tribulations of their Viking ancestors, who forged their very identities amidst the lush forests and majestic fjords, and by perpetuating their heritage through sagas, oral traditions, customs, and sacred landmarks, present-day Swedes embark on a journey of self-cultivation, fortifying themselves with resilience, responsibility, and community-focused virtues that have been proven to enhance societal well-being.

Indeed, the legacy of the Vikings still contains invaluable lessons for navigating the tumultuous seas of disruptive times. While Faustian bargains may tempt us with the allure of quick and effortless success, it is in the pursuit of balance, continuity, and the courage to confront life's enigmas head-on that true prosperity lies. The sagacious Swedes understand this inherently, for their Viking inheritance has bestowed upon them a wealth of wisdom that transcends time and space.

The Vikings, with their insatiable hunger for exploration and adventure, held a profound understanding of the human spirit and its unyielding yearning for growth. Their unwavering determination to defy mediocrity and embrace the unknown allowed them to leave an indelible mark on history, shaping the course of civilizations and inspiring countless generations to come. The Viking ethos compels us to overthrow the shackles of complacency and embrace the challenges that lie before us, for it is through adversity that we discover the depths of our character and carve our destinies.

Additionally, the Viking spirit of communal solidarity serves as a cornerstone for societal well-being. Throughout their tumultuous history, the Vikings relied on their close-knit communities to navigate treacherous waters and survive the harshest of circumstances. This communally-centered approach fostered a deep sense of connection and mutual responsibility amongst individuals, ensuring their collective welfare and fostering a spirit of empathy and support. These virtues passed down through the ages, continue to guide modern-day Swedes, reminding them of the crucial importance of nurturing strong bonds within their communities and anchoring themselves in a shared sense of purpose and responsibility.

However, the lessons derived from the Vikings extend beyond mere resilience and camaraderie. The Norse ancestors also instilled in their descendants a profound respect for nature and a deep understanding of their intricate relationship with the environment. The Vikings, who roamed the lands in harmony with their natural surroundings, honored the forests and fjords that sustained them, recognizing the interdependence between humanity and the ecosystems that surround us. This inherent ecological wisdom encourages modern-day Swedes to embrace sustainable practices and stewardship, ensuring the preservation of natural resources for future generations.

In an era marked by rapid technological advances and the alluring promises of convenience, the Viking legacy stands as a testament to the enduring power of tradition. While the world evolves at an unprecedented pace, the timeless wisdom encapsulated in the sagas and oral traditions of the Vikings reminds us of the unwavering importance of preserving our cultural heritage. By immersing themselves in the tales of yore, Swedes can forge a profound connection with their roots, grounding themselves in a rich tapestry of stories, traditions, and customs that have weathered the ebbs and flows of time.

It is undeniable that the world is in a perpetual state of flux, with uncertainty lurking around every corner. In times of such profound uncertainty, the lessons drawn from the Viking legacy assume an even greater significance. The Vikings were masters of adapting to adversity, of maneuvering through the stormiest of seas with a resolute resolve. Likewise, modern-day Swedes carry within them this ancestral strength, honed through generations of resilience and courage.

The living cultural tie to the Viking-era foundations provides Sweden with an invaluable psychological anchor and a wellspring of collective pride. In the face of the disruptive forces of globalization, the enduring spirit fostered in Scandinavia's north offers stability and continuity. By embracing the wisdom encapsulated in their Viking heritage, modern Swedes cultivate the virtues necessary for societal well-being: resilience, responsibility, and community-focused values. In our Faustian age, where shortcuts may entice and mislead, the lessons imparted by the Vikings remind us that it is balance, continuity, and the audacity to confront the mysteries of life with courage that ultimately pave the path toward sustainable prosperity. It is in this recognition that the Swedes discover the wisdom they need to thrive in an ever-changing world, drawing strength from the timeless lessons of their Viking ancestry.

Sweden Archaeological Discoveries

The rugged coasts and forested interior of what we now recognize as Sweden conceal cultural treasures that have illuminated the character of those hardy souls who once roamed this northern realm. Through diligent excavation and interpretation, archaeologists have unearthed artifacts that speak to the industrious spirit, fearsome prowess in battle, and creative artistic flair of the Vikings who called this harsh yet bountiful land home.

One of the most fascinating and enlightening discoveries that offer us a glimpse into the complex societal dynamics, economic networks, and profound religious beliefs of the Viking civilization is unquestionably the trading center of Birka, situated on the island of Björkö, adjacent to the contemporary city of Stockholm. Since the commencement of extensive excavations at Birka in the 1870s, an array of invaluable relics, ranging from intricate jewelry and formidable weapons to remnants of opulent halls and over a thousand graves, have unveiled remarkable insights into this ancient Norse settlement. Beyond its mere function as a bustling marketplace, the magnitude and arrangement of Birka suggest its crucial role as an administrative hub, with clearly demarcated areas for diverse crafts, residences of varying prestige, and dedicated spaces for sacred rituals and burial ceremonies.

Through the meticulous excavation efforts and the rebirth of long-buried artifacts, we are presented with a multidimensional portrait of the Vikings' social fabric meticulously woven together on the shores of Birka. As we delve into this intricate tapestry, we can appreciate the multifaceted nature of the Viking society and the intertwinement of their various spheres of existence.

First and foremost, the sheer magnitude of Birka speaks volumes about its significance, both as a commercial nexus and as an administrative and political stronghold. The bustling hub sprawls across the landscape, intricately designed to accommodate the multifarious activities that transpired within its vibrant confines. The delineation of distinct zones within the settlement showcases the meticulous planning and organization that underpin Viking society. Birka was much more than a marketplace, embracing a multifaceted role in the lives of its inhabitants.

One of the prominent aspects elucidated by the excavations is the allocation of space for craft production. The presence of designated areas for various specialized crafts signals the specialization and division of labor inherent in the Viking society. Smiths, potters, weavers, and other skilled artisans were allocated separate spaces to ply their trades, weaving together the intricate fabric of the Viking economy. The discovery of workshops, tools, and remnants of the goods they produced attest to their pivotal role in sustaining both the local economy and the broader Viking world.

Furthermore, Birka's layout reveals a profound concern for the social structure and hierarchy prevalent in Viking society. The discernible residential zones, characterized by varying sizes and opulence of the houses, provide valuable insights into the socio-economic stratification inherent in the settlement. The dwellings of the wealthy and powerful, resplendent with their intricate woodwork and lavish decoration, stand in stark contrast to the modest abodes of the lower strata of society. The unequal distribution of wealth and status is unmistakable and subtly mirrored within the layout of the settlement itself.

Equally significant is the establishment of designated spaces for religious ceremonies and burial practices. Within the intricate fabric of Birka, we discover areas dedicated to the worship of the gods, the performance of sacred rituals, and the commemoration of the deceased. The presence of grave sites, some grandiose with elaborate grave goods and others more modest, speaks to the profound significance the Vikings attributed to the afterlife and the commemoration of their ancestors. The inclusion of such sacred spaces within the settlement exemplifies the intimate bond between the religious and communal life of the Vikings.

As we delve deeper into the graves unearthed in Birka, we encounter a treasure trove of information about the personal and collective identities of its inhabitants. The varied burial customs, the intricate grave goods, and the positions in which the bodies were interred all speak to the rich tapestry of beliefs and traditions that shaped Viking society. By studying these burial practices, we gain invaluable insights into the complex web of religious convictions, social status, and cultural values that governed the daily lives of the Vikings.

In the enigmatic and elaborate jewelry discovered in

Birka, we find a testament to the Vikings' aesthetic sophistication. The craftsmanship and intricacy displayed in the bracelets, necklaces, and brooches evidence their impeccable skill and artistic sensibilities. These adornments serve not only as expressions of personal style but also as symbols of status and prestige. The Vikings' appreciation for beauty and their desire to elevate their social standing through opulent displays further illuminate the profound interplay between material culture and social identity within Birka and, by extension, Viking civilization as a whole.

As we piece together the discoveries from Birka, a remarkable and extraordinarily detailed portrait of the Viking world emerges. The settlement's function as a bustling trade center, an administrative hub, and a site of intricate religious practices unveils a society intricate in its socio-economic organization and spirituality. The complexity and interconnectedness of the various facets of Viking life showcased at Birka attest to a society whose vitality, resilience, and cultural richness continue to capture our imagination centuries later.

Within the sprawling necropolis, archaeologists have encountered graves outfitted with all manner of provisions for the afterlife journey, as well as hints at the social ranking of the deceased. Wealthy traders and officials were interred with horses, costly armaments, delicately crafted brooches, and strings of beads, reflecting their elevated position within the hierarchical clan system. More modest burials contained more basic equipment and provisions, though even the lower classes were apt to be sent off with a cherished weapon, suggesting a warrior ethos pervaded Viking society across strata. Perhaps most evocative are the skeletons of sacrifice victims discovered within the town perimeter, strong evidence that fearful pre-Christian rituals persisted even in this cosmopolitan crossroads where diverse cultural influences intermingled.

Birka's status as a center of commerce is corroborated by artifacts bearing distinctly non-Scandinavian traces, such as Arab dirhams and Anglo-Saxon coins recovered amidst the ruins. Its location at the intersection of river routes connecting inland forests and agricultural settlements to the Baltic Sea lanes made it a logical hub for exchanging furs, walrus ivory, wax, and hides from the north for luxuries from abroad. The diversity of cultures encountered here may help explain why the Vikings who ruled from Birka were among the last holdouts against the tide of Christianity sweeping across Europe - they had developed a taste for intellectual and material goods from many lands and were slow to abandon their ancestral spiritual traditions.

Across the forests and inland waterways of central Sweden lies another settlement site whose uncovered riches illuminate the ingenuity and craftsmanship for which Vikings were renowned - Hemse on the island of Gotland. Extensive man-made mounds and remnants of buildings hint that this too was a significant local center, perhaps involved in organizing agricultural production and craft specialization for trade. Most impressive are the stone ship settings and elaborate picture stones carved with scenes of warriors, festivities, and mythical beasts that once lined the paths and boundaries of the village.

Through careful reconstruction, archaeologists have pieced together depictions of formidable longships laden with armed crewmen, contextual clues that these maritime-oriented people invested their craft not just with practical importance but deep cultural and symbolic meaning. The pictorial stones convey sophisticated metaphors and allusions to Norse myths, evidence that an intricate oral literary tradition coexisted alongside fighting prowess and commercial success. At Hemse, inhabitants drew upon and celebrated their heritage not just through functional objects but decorative art that still maintains the capacity to astonish modern viewers with its creative virtuosity. Its imagery resonated with rituals of courage, competition, and voyaging that were fundamentals of Viking psychology and social bonds.

Moving inland, the area surrounding Lake Mälar was a pivotal center of power formation during the Viking Age, with the town of Birka and its rival settlement of Sigtuna perched on opposite shores. Much can be gleaned about governance and upper-class residences from the royal manor and assembly site uncovered at Håga, surrounded by signs of skilled crafts and productive farming. Within its outer enclosure were grand timber longhouses and several parallel rows of smaller dwellings for dependents or servants, a layout suggestive of ranked social roles. But most enlightening was the presence of two partially reconstructed sacrificial groves, complete with remains of sacrificed animals, musical instruments, and gaming pieces.

In examining the historical remnants of the Viking era, a fascinating revelation emerges that challenges our preconceived notions of the role and nature of rulers during that time. Contrary to the conventional image of these leaders as merely political and military strong-men, it becomes increasingly apparent that they held a multifaceted role, one that encompassed the responsibilities of ritual priests as well. These rulers, occupying the highest echelons of Viking command chains, were entrusted with the sacred task of mediating between the people and the gods.

This newfound understanding is not merely the result of conjecture but rather is supported by concrete evidence, particularly the material culture associated with sacrificial ceremonies. It is through the objects and artifacts left behind that we gain insight into the spiritual practices and belief systems that permeated Viking society. Among these significant findings are gaming pieces, which provide undeniable indications of the presence of competitive gambling dedicated to the gods. These gaming pieces, often intricately crafted and adorned, served not only as tools for entertainment but also as vessels for divine communication.

The significance of these gaming pieces extends far beyond their recreational value. They illuminate the interwoven nature of spirituality, honor competitions, and communal bonds within the upper echelons of Viking authority. Through these sacred games, rulers sought to impart a sense of divine purpose to their actions and decisions, instilling within their subjects a shared understanding of the importance of moral conduct and spiritual well-being.

It is crucial to recognize that Viking society was not solely shaped by political and military might. True authority in this theocratic society derived from the maintenance of righteous relations with the unseen forces that were deemed essential for community welfare and success in battle. Rulers were not merely wielding power for power's sake; they were guardians of a sacred pact between the mortal realm and the divine. This recognition fundamentally alters our perception of Viking rulers, portraying them as spiritual leaders who possessed a profound understanding of the intrinsic connection between the material and the spiritual.

As we delve deeper into the intricate tapestry of Viking culture, we encounter two distinct yet complementary exemplars: Birka and Håga. These archaeological sites offer distinct glimpses into the mindset and values of the Viking elite, each bearing a unique character reflective of their respective time and context.

In the vast and enigmatic lands of Sweden, remnants of a bygone era still echo the tales of the mighty Norsemen. Delving into the depths of these lands, one can uncover a treasure trove of relics, hiding within their ancient folds the secrets of livelihoods, worldviews, and activities that formed the very essence of Viking identity. These artifacts, despite being scantily documented in the annals of history, offer us a glimpse into the rich tapestry of Viking life, their beliefs, and the strategies they employed to establish their dominance.

One such intriguing discovery lies in the region surrounding Uppsala, a site that exudes an aura of grandiosity and spirituality. As one traverses the approach to Uppsala, the remnants of fortress-like structures and protective stakes emerge from the earth, providing a tantalizing clue to the significance of this place. Christian chronicles, penned centuries after the Viking era, inform us of the great sacrifices that took place here yearly, speaking to the sacred nature of the Uppsala environs. These sources, influenced by the advent of Christianity, shed light on the reverence with which the Norse held this hallowed ground, illuminating the deep connection between their religious beliefs and the physical landscape they inhabited.

The notion of sacrifice, permeating through the hearts and minds of the Norse, becomes all the more poignant as we investigate the sites of Lujavaara and Orust.

These locales, through the remnants of furnaces and smelting debris, provide us with a window into the intensive iron production that underpinned the military might and commercial prowess of the Vikings. To truly fathom the wealth and power they amassed, we must acknowledge the arduous and collaborative labor that ensued in extracting and working these natural resources. The Viking civilization, it seems, thrived on the backbreaking toil of forging iron, a testament to their ingenuity and industriousness.

As we delve further into the narrative of Viking livelihood, the portrait of empowerment and ingenuity becomes even more pronounced. Military might, engrained deep within the core of Viking identity, necessitated a comprehensive understanding of the interconnectedness between trade and wealth. The legendary Viking longships, the feathers in their cap if you will, elegantly sailed across vast oceans, forging lucrative trade alliances, and reaping the spoils of exploration. Yet, we must not be seduced by the romantic notion of adventuring Vikings; their success stemmed from the meticulous extraction and utilization of natural resources at their disposal. Utilizing their ironworking prowess, they constructed these mighty vessels to seamlessly navigate treacherous waters and support their ambitious trading endeavors.

However, it is crucial to ponder the metaphysical aspects of Viking life as well. The material wealth and power they amassed was not simply for its own sake but rather to establish a sense of order and structure in their world, and perhaps even to please the gods. The Vikings, deeply influenced by their pagan beliefs, sought to forge a profound connection between the temporal and the divine. In their quest for cosmic harmony, they erected grand burial sites, such as the famous Viking ship burials, intricate stone monuments, and enigmatic rune stones. These necropolises reflect their reverence for the cycle of life and death, symbolizing their belief in a glorious afterlife reserved for those who lived valiantly and honorably.

In essence, these relics scattered across the Swedish landscape form an intricate tapestry, woven by the hands and minds of the Vikings themselves. They offer us a gateway into understanding not only the physical activities and strategies that molded the Viking civilization but also the deeply ingrained values and beliefs that underpinned their existence. By unearthing these artifacts, we grasp the profound impact of collaboration, expressed through arduous labor, on the development of Viking power and wealth. Beyond material gains, we peer into the spiritual fabric of their lives, where sacrifice and reverence for the divine played a fundamental role.

Thus, the story of the Norsemen is not merely one of plunder and conquest, as often portrayed, but rather a tale of resilience and resourcefulness, rooted in a profound symbiosis with nature and gods. These relics, through their silent testimony, beckon us to voyage alongside the Vikings on their tumultuous journey, to reimagine their triumphs and hardships, and to redraw the boundaries of our understanding of this illustrious civilization. Let us brave these uncharted territories, delving into the depths of history, and embarking upon an intellectual voyage where the ghosts of the past whisper their tales, allowing us to unravel the mysteries that lie dormant within the Swedish soil.

Across the agricultural landscape spread farm sites like Överhogdal which reveal how diverse outputs were achieved via crop cultivation, animal grazing, and dairying - self-sufficiency was a necessity in the seasonal boreal climate. Port facilities such as Kaupang highlighted the logistical role in coordinating goods between inland, coastal, and open sea zones which was requisite for Viking commercial success. Piece by painstaking piece, archaeology has amplified our comprehension of the material, economic, and administrative sophistication that allowed Scandinavian warriors and explorers to flourish as a distinct, expansive yet cohesive society.

While runestones, poems, and pictorial artworks give some insight into the psychological dimensions of Viking life, the most evocative artifacts are those that bring us face-to-face with individual Vikings themselves. Across gravesites, scientists have accessed untold numbers of skeletons offering a nuanced understanding of health, nutrition, activities, and even social roles like that of the famous Birka "warrior woman" whose remains were accompanied by arms befitting a combative persona unafraid to defy gender strictures. Cranial and dental analyses provide windows into lifelong occupations and lived experiences, from warriors exhibiting signs of head trauma to craftspeople with bone spurs and enamel degeneration from tool use.

In the grand tapestry of human history, few figures have captured our imagination as vividly and enduringly as the Vikings. These seafaring warriors and traders from the chilly Nordic regions have etched themselves into our collective consciousness, conjuring images of fearsome longships, brutal raids, and bloody battles. Yet beneath this popular caricature lies a more nuanced and complex truth, unearthed by recent genetic research on ancient Scandinavian DNA extracted from burial grounds.

What this research has revealed is nothing short of remarkable—it paints a picture of ancestral ties and migratory patterns on a scale that was once unfathomable to earlier generations. In essence, the genetic evidence points to the fact that Viking expansion had profound and far-reaching effects, reshaping not only the demographics of the settler zones such as Ireland, England, and Iceland but also the very fabric of their ancestral homelands by incorporating new bloodlines.

Gone are the days when we could simplistically view the Vikings as mere raiders and traders, preoccupied solely with sowing chaos and acquiring wealth. Instead, we now understand them as a diverse and dynamic group of settlers and pioneers. They frequently intermingled and intermarried with local populations, forging symbiotic relationships that spanned the vast expanses from Greenland to Russia. The Vikings played a pivotal role in becoming the ancestors of modern-day descendants across Europe and North America, leaving an indelible mark on the genetic landscape of these regions.

To comprehend the magnitude of this revelation, let us consider a recent DNA analysis from a 10th-century farm in Estonia. The findings were nothing short of astonishing, as they revealed that the inhabitants of this farm not only had genetic ties to Scandinavia but also Finland and Russia. This singular example represents a microcosm of a fluid and heterogeneous social reality that was interconnected on both biological and cultural levels.

The implications of these genetic discoveries reverberate far beyond the academic realm. They challenge elements of our understanding of Viking culture, forcing us to reconsider long-held assumptions about these intrepid explorers. We must grapple with the realization that the Vikings were not a monolithic entity, but a vibrant tapestry woven together by diverse threads of DNA, cultural exchange, and adaptation.

The concept of Viking identity, once fiercely tethered to ethnocentrism and a narrow definition of belonging, now faces the daunting task of encompassing the rich complexity and diversity uncovered by genetics. Hence, the very notion of what it means to be a descendant of the Vikings has been radically altered. A newfound respect for the malleability of identity is demanded, as the Vikings transcend the confines of national borders and expand the parameters of shared ancestry.

While the romanticized image of a lone Viking hero, exuding strength and battling adversity, may still hold sway in our collective imagination, it is crucial to recognize that this narrow representation fails to capture the full breadth and depth of Viking influence. The Vikings were much more than marauding mariners—they were also architects of cultural exchange, pioneers of exploration, and catalysts of genetic diversity.

As we delve deeper into the genetic treasure trove of ancient Scandinavian DNA, it becomes apparent that the Vikings were not confined to plundering and pillaging. They were, in fact, intrepid settlers who ventured far and wide, eager to carve out new homes for themselves and their descendants. They forged connections and alliances with indigenous populations, leaving their mark not only on the land they conquered but also on the very genetic makeup of those they encountered.

It is in the genetic admixture resulting from these interminglings that we see the true legacy of the Vikings. Today, modern-day descendants across Europe and North America bear witness to this enduring imprint. The DNA passed down through generations serves as a living testament to the migratory paths, intermarriages, and cultural syntheses that occurred during this transformative era.

In this ever-changing landscape of historical understanding, we must resist the temptation to reduce the Vikings to simplistic caricatures. Their story is one of complexity, diversity, and resilience. To appreciate the full scope of their impact, we must embrace the interdisciplinary approach, weaving together genetic research, historical narratives, linguistic analysis, and archaeological findings to paint a more holistic and accurate picture.

Through unearthing tangible goods and human skeletal remains, Swedish archaeology has elevated our perspective of the Vikings from daring raiders to a complex, far-flung yet tightly-knit network of traders, farmers, craftspeople, and empire-builders. They forged a sophisticated culture from harsh northern environs through skills in seafaring, metallurgy, crafts, ritual, and governance - all while developing far-flung economic and social interactions that reshaped the genetic and cultural structure of much of Europe and North America. Though their society was eventually transformed by Christianization and centralization of kingdoms, the spirit of rugged independence, technical innovation, and close community ties that flourished under adversity continue to shape the Swedish national character and influence globalized modernity. Through diligent excavation and the increasingly powerful lens of DNA analysis, archaeology brings us face-to-face with individual Vikings and vividly portrays a people who defied harsh environs to spread their genes and memes across oceans through courage, creativity, and communal solidarity. Their saga truly deserves the attention it continues to receive from those seeking to comprehend humanity's endless capacity for resilience, exploration, and cultural blossoming even under life's most challenging of conditions.

Influence on Swedish Institutions

The Vikings, with their undying spirit of adventure, self-sufficiency, and commitment to egalitarianism, profoundly influenced Swedish society and governance, leaving behind an extraordinary legacy that reverberates through history until this very day. As the Vikings transitioned from their seafaring lifestyle to a more settled agrarian society during the late Iron Age, they birthed the foundations of some of the earliest representative assemblies and judicial gatherings known as "things." These early institutions paved the way for the establishment of Sweden's modern parliamentary democracy, which has continued to flourish and evolve over the centuries. The Viking ethos of independence, consensus-building, and societal cohesion continues to be cherished by Swedes, as these values are deeply intertwined with their Viking heritage.

The transition of the Vikings to an agrarian society marked a significant turning point in their history. No longer solely reliant on plundering and raiding, the Vikings began cultivating the soil and embracing a more sedentary way of life. This transition allowed for the development of settled communities, fostering the emergence of organized governance systems that reflected the principles upheld by the Vikings.

One crucial aspect of Viking society that contributed to their legacy of Swedish governance was their embrace of early representative assemblies and judgment gatherings known as "things." These were local assemblies where societal matters were discussed and resolved through open discussions and democratic decision-making processes. The participants, including free men, landowners, and chieftains, would convene at these gatherings to address legal disputes, forge alliances, and make decisions concerning the greater welfare of their community.

The concept of the "thing" symbolized the Viking commitment to egalitarian ideals, as it provided every member of the community with an equal opportunity to voice their concerns and participate in the decision-making process. This early practice of inclusive governance profoundly influenced the development of Swedish society, solidifying the belief in the importance of representation and open dialogue that remains at the core of their modern parliamentary democracy.

As these Viking-era assemblies evolved and merged with Christian influences, they eventually gave birth to Sweden's Riksdag, or Parliament, which remains the nation's highest legislative body to this day. The

Riksdag, with its multi-party system and deliberative approach to governance, embodies the Viking principles of consensus-building, where varying viewpoints are considered before critical decisions are made. This commitment to consensus propels Sweden towards a society rooted in shared values and mutual understanding.

Sweden's Viking heritage continues to shape its governance structure in more subtle ways as well. The Vikings were renowned for their self-reliance, individualism, and personal agency. These characteristics, deeply ingrained in their culture, have transcended the sands of time and continue to influence the Swedish approach to governance and society.

The notion of self-reliance emphasized by the Vikings manifests itself in the Swedish social welfare system, which seeks to empower individuals and ensure they are self-sufficient. Rather than fostering a dependency culture, Sweden's social programs aim to provide citizens with the support and means necessary to navigate life independently. This commitment to self-empowerment resonates with the Viking spirit of personal agency, where individuals take responsibility for their actions and livelihood.

Furthermore, the Viking ethos of egalitarianism still echoes through Swedish society. In Viking times, wealth and power were not solely concentrated in the hands of the few but were more evenly distributed throughout the community. This ideology of egalitarianism, where no individual's worth is determined solely by their social status, continues to shape Swedish society's perception of equality and social justice.

Sweden's dedication to gender equality, for instance, finds its roots in its Viking inheritance. The Norse sagas often depicted shieldmaidens and strong female characters, highlighting the societal acceptance of women's competence and capacity to participate in traditionally male-dominated realms. This egalitarian mindset has permeated Swedish culture, leading to progressive policies and attitudes towards gender roles, from gender-inclusive language to significant representation of women in politics and business.

Another crucial aspect of Viking heritage that resonates with modern Swedish governance is their community-focused mentality. The Vikings understood the intrinsic value of social cohesion and collaboration, knowing that working together was essential for the survival and prosperity of their communities.

This collective mindset is evident in the Swedish value placed on consensus-building and cooperation. Decision-making processes in Sweden often involve extensive consultations and negotiations, allowing for the inclusion of various perspectives and ensuring a sense of collective ownership over the outcomes. By valuing consensus and social cohesion, Sweden cultivates a harmonious society that thrives on the well-being of its citizens.

The Vikings left an indelible mark on the foundations of Swedish law, as their influence resonated through the annals of history. Embedded within their societal structure were the thing assemblies, which not only functioned as a symbol of unity but also as crucial law courts. It is within these ancient assemblies that we can trace the origins of many legal principles and practices that would come to shape Sweden's legal system.

One can hardly overlook the Vikings' unwavering commitment to oral tradition, as it stood at the very heart of their culture. This emphasis on oral history extended to legal matters as well, permeating the realm of dispute resolution. The Vikings recognized the power and importance of spoken words, as they crafted narratives and arguments to unveil the truth. Oral tradition played a fundamental role in their law courts, where testimonies were given through spoken words and aural debates ensued.

Law, to the Vikings, was not a static and rigid entity; instead, it thrived on the dynamic interplay of precedent. The importance placed on past decisions and outcomes within the thing assemblies lent a sense of continuity and guidance to their legal system. Decisions made by their chieftains and elders became case studies that future disputes were evaluated against. Precedent, seen as a reflection of accumulated wisdom and communal values, offered a framework for contextualizing and resolving legal conflicts.

The tenets of Viking justice, comprising pragmatism and proportionality, epitomized their approach to law and order. The Vikings embraced a practical mindset, understanding that the application of justice must align with the realities of the community. This pragmatism, deeply ingrained in their societal fabric, greatly influenced the development of Swedish law. Over the centuries, as Sweden's legal system took shape, the principles of pragmatism and proportionality persisted, reflecting the enduring legacy of the Vikings.

Swedish law, despite evolving and undergoing codification, has remained deeply rooted in Viking traditions. The focus on pragmatism, proportionality, and communal welfare has persisted through the ages, transcending the passage of time. Advocating for the greater good of the community has always been central, aligning with the Vikings' deep-seated values. Whether it be the resolution of disputes, the imposition of penalties, or the crafting of legislation, Swedish law seeks to strike a delicate balance that upholds justice while attending to the collective well-being.

In exploring the intricate facets of Viking influence on Swedish law, we unearth an ethical framework that resonates across the ages. The Vikings' commitment to justice did not merely revolve around individual rights and retribution but rather encompassed the greater ideals of communal welfare and prosperity. It is this holistic perspective that served as the backbone of their legal system, one that prioritized the sustenance of harmony and the promotion of societal welfare.

And so, we discover that the Viking impact on Swedish law extends far beyond the realm of legal principles. Their influence stretches into the very essence of Swedish society, shaping the nation's values, customs, and norms. Through their thing assemblies, the Vikings fostered a sense of collective responsibility and participation, a characteristic that has persisted and thrived in the fabric of Swedish democracy.

In the realm of education, the Vikings, with their rich and fascinating history, bestowed upon us a set of values that continue to shape Sweden's educational system to this very day. Through their expeditions, trade routes, and settlements, the Vikings exemplified skill, adaptability, and the importance of imparting practical knowledge to the younger generation. These values, deeply rooted in their culture, have had a lasting impact on the Swedish emphasis on egalitarian and comprehensive education, which places equal importance on both academic and vocational skills.

In Sweden, education is not limited to the transmission of knowledge alone, but rather, it strives to foster independence, creativity, and social responsibility in students. These qualities, which served the Vikings well as they ventured into new territories, exploring the unknown and establishing trade networks, are still highly valued in Swedish society today. The Vikings' legacy of nurturing these traits has contributed greatly to the Swedish mindset and their ability to adapt to changing circumstances, ensuring both individual growth and social cohesion.

While Sweden's educational system has undergone modernization over the years, the core values instilled by the Vikings have remained steadfast. The Vikings were known for their self-reliance, a characteristic deeply ingrained in Swedish society. Self-reliance empowers individuals to take charge of their learning and development, allowing them to embrace challenges with confidence and resilience. This value is reflected in the educational system's emphasis on empowering students and encouraging their active participation in the learning process.

In addition to self-reliance, consensus-building is

another cornerstone of Swedish society that can be traced back to the Vikings' influence. The Vikings, as seafaring people, understood the importance of collaboration and teamwork to navigate vast oceans and establish successful settlements. This spirit of cooperation has permeated Swedish culture, and it is reflected in their education system, which encourages students to work together, exchange ideas, and find consensus through open and respectful dialogue.

The pragmatic nature of the Vikings is also deeply rooted in Swedish society. Pragmatism, as exemplified by the Vikings, involves a practical approach to problem-solving and decision-making. It emphasizes the importance of adapting to new situations and using available resources efficiently. This pragmatic mindset carried forward from the Viking era, is reflected in the Swedish educational system, which strives to provide students with practical skills that can be applied in real-world situations, preparing them for the challenges they will face as adults.

The Vikings' commitment to social cohesion, evident in their strong sense of community and responsibility towards one another, continues to shape Sweden's educational system today. Swedish schools aim to cultivate not only academic excellence but also social responsibility. This involves instilling values such as empathy, compassion, and respect for others. By fostering a sense of social responsibility, Swedish education seeks to create well-rounded citizens who contribute positively to society as a whole.

It is undeniable that the pioneering spirit of the Vikings has left a profound and enduring mark on Swedish institutions and the national character. The values of skill, adaptability, and imparting practical knowledge are deeply ingrained in the educational fabric of Sweden. These values, along with self-reliance, consensus, pragmatism, and social cohesion, continue to shape not only the education system but also the political and legal systems of the country.

Cultural Impact in Modern Sweden

In the grand tapestry of history, modern Sweden stands as a nation deeply rooted in its Viking heritage. It is a land where the echoes of courageous explorers and skilled warriors continue to reverberate through the hearts and minds of its inhabitants. Proudly cherishing their adventurous spirit and profound influence, the people of Sweden have taken it upon themselves to preserve, celebrate, and propagate the essence of their Viking ancestry.

At the very core of modern Swedish culture lies an unwavering appreciation for the boundless courage that characterized the Vikings. These intrepid seafarers fearlessly set sail into uncharted waters, charting new territories and bringing their indomitable spirit to shores far and wide. This courageous disposition is not confined to the annals of history but continues to shape the national character of Sweden. From the exploration of uncharted territories to the pursuit of bold visions, the Swedes carry forth the torch of courage, refusing to be shackled by the constraints of uncertainty and fear.

In the realm of Swedish culture, a profound sense of pride permeates society when it comes to safeguarding and commemorating the illustrious Viking heritage. Across the vast expanse of this nation, one can discover an abundance of reminders hailing from an era that continues to shape the national character through its audacious and intrepid spirit. Sweden's commitment to preserving this rich tapestry of history is truly remarkable, most evident in its multitude of museums that meticulously curate and display exhibits dedicated to the Viking Age. These institutions serve as sacred vessels of knowledge, vividly breathing life into a bygone era and educating visitors about the remarkable achievements and intricate way of life of these indomitable seafarers.

Among the myriad cultural centers that dot Sweden's landscape, it is within the hallowed halls of museums where the Viking Age manifests with unparalleled vivacity. These institutions of enlightenment effortlessly transcend the barriers of time, immersing visitors in a captivating journey through history. Authentic artifacts, meticulously preserved and gracefully showcased, serve as tangible portals to a world untamed by modernity. Here, admirers of history are greeted by stunning metalwork, intricate weaponry, and awe-inspiring jewelry, all forged and cherished by the hands of Viking craftsmen. These treasures, perhaps once plundered from distant shores, now bear testament to the indomitable spirit of the Viking people and their ceaseless quest for exploration, conquest, and spiritual reverence.

As one meanders through these hallowed halls, a sense of profound respect and admiration fills the air. The legacy left behind by the Vikings resonates deeply within the collective consciousness of the Swedish people, who keenly understand the profound impact these seafaring warriors had on their nation's identity. Far from being mere marauders and doers of violence, the Vikings embodied a unique fusion of intellectual curiosity, artistic prowess, and intrepid exploration. Engaging with the exhibits, one begins to appreciate the multifaceted nature of these Scandinavian pioneers and the myriad of contributions they made to European civilization.

Venturing further into the cultural tapestry of Sweden,

one finds captivating historical sites that offer immersive glimpses into actual Viking settlements. Birka, a renowned archeological site on the island of Björkö, beckons visitors with its authentic reconstruction of Viking-era buildings. Amidst these meticulously crafted structures, countless stories whisper from the past, offering fleeting insights into the daily triumphs, challenges, and rituals of Viking life. This open-air museum, nestled within a breathtaking natural landscape, serves as a window into the soul of a people whose ingenuity and tenacity shaped the very essence of the Swedish nation.

Similarly, Hedeby, located in present-day Germany, stands as a monumental testament to Viking presence beyond the shores of Sweden. Once a bustling trade hub, Hedeby witnessed the convergence of various cultures and the forging of crucial alliances. Today, this ancient settlement provides an invaluable vantage point into a thriving community that thrived on maritime trade, craftsmanship, and cultural exchange. Visitors to Hedeby can explore reconstructed Viking homes and workshops, gaining a profound sense of the ingenuity, resilience, and interconnectedness that characterized Viking society. As one walks in the footsteps of these seafaring merchants, an imperative question emerges: What can we glean from the Vikings that can inspire our contemporary world?

Embracing and celebrating the Viking legacy is not limited to historians, academics, or enthusiasts alone. Swedish society as a whole is deeply permeated by the lasting impact of the Viking Age. From art and literature to cuisine and architecture, echoes of Viking culture reverberate within the very fabric of Swedish daily life. The flamboyant and distinctively patterned textiles reflecting Norse aesthetics adorn contemporary homes and fashion, bridging a vast temporal chasm. Through these deliberate nods to the past, both subtle and overt, Swedes honor their Viking forebears, ensuring their memory continues to thrive amidst the ever-shifting sands of time.

In examining the profound influence of the Viking heritage, one must not overlook the philosophical significance embedded within their ethos. These ancient tales serve as archetypes, resonating deeply within the collective unconsciousness of individuals and societies alike. The mythic sagas of the Viking Age, filled with stories of heroism, exploration, and constant striving, offer a profound source of inspiration and guidance for contemporary individuals seeking meaning and purpose.

Just as ancient narratives provided moral guidance for the Vikings, resolute individuals today can glean valuable lessons from their indomitable spirit. The story of the Vikings goes far beyond their fearsome reputation; it encapsulates resilience in the face of adversity, the pursuit of knowledge in the unknown, and a valiant quest for personal growth. The Vikings, driven by an insatiable curiosity, set sail upon treacherous waters, fervently seeking new horizons. This audacious spirit, rooted in a thirst for knowledge and personal growth, pulses within the hearts of modern individuals who endeavor to push boundaries and transcend limitations.

Moreover, the Viking spirit encompasses the idea of embracing challenges and confronting the unknown. It is through their relentless exploration and daring exploits that the Vikings dismantled the perceived boundaries of their age. The blue vastness of the ocean, studded with uncertainty and peril, became a canvas upon which they painted their destinies. In an era still grappling with its uncharted waters, with increasingly complex socio-political landscapes and overarching uncertainty, the lessons of the Vikings can be viewed as guiding beacons of resilience and adaptability.

Festivals play a vital role in the preservation and perpetuation of Viking traditions and cultural heritage. These captivating events serve as vibrant platforms that transport attendees back in time, connecting them to the pre-Christian solstice celebrations of their Viking ancestors. The Midsummer festival held in Uppsala, Sweden, for instance, epitomizes the enduring bond between the modern Swedes and their Viking roots.

At the heart of Uppsala's Midsummer festival lies a profound acknowledgment of the solstice rites that were once performed by the ancient Norse inhabitants of Scandinavia. The festival acts as a tribute to these primordial customs, honoring the mystical power of the summer solstice and its significance within Viking cosmology. By embracing these traditions, the festival weaves together the threads of the past and the present, forming a tapestry of cultural continuity.

One particularly spectacular aspect of the festival is the Viking Market held in Stockholm. This gathering serves as a grand spectacle, offering a captivating glimpse into the daily lives and activities of the mighty Norse warriors. Skilled reenactors adeptly demonstrate ancient Viking crafts, such as blacksmithing, woodworking, and pottery, immersing attendees in the artisanal techniques and creative prowess of their Viking ancestors. Moreover, combat demonstrations allow visitors to witness the skillful prowess and ferocity displayed in the fierce Viking battles of yore.

However, it is not just in these bustling urban hubs

where Viking traditions manifest themselves. In rural areas of Scandinavia, local Leidang festivals provide a unique opportunity to experience the revival of the Viking military assembly and defense system. These gatherings symbolize the unwavering communal spirit that was prevalent during Viking times, as participants joined forces to recreate the practices of their militaristic forefathers. Through simulated battles and strategic maneuvers, attendees not only gain insights into Viking military tactics but also forge bonds of camaraderie and solidarity reminiscent of the Viking spirit.

To ensure the continuity of Viking traditions, it is crucial to engage and inspire future generations. Educational programs offered at places like Sweden's

Viking Village serve as invaluable resources for imparting knowledge about Viking culture to the young. By integrating history lessons with interactive experiences, these programs ignite the curiosity and imagination of the youth, allowing them to step into the shoes of their Viking ancestors. Through hands-on activities like sword forging, shield painting, and traditional cooking, the younger generation not only gains practical skills but also becomes intimately acquainted with the intricate details of Viking life.

Moreover, educational programs in Viking Villages foster an understanding of Viking values, instilling in young minds a deep appreciation for qualities such as honor, bravery, and the pursuit of knowledge. By embodying these principles, the younger generation discovers the timeless relevance of Viking culture and its potential to shape their own lives positively.

The profound impacts of Viking influences on Swedish arts and media have undoubtedly left an indelible mark throughout the centuries. From the ancient Eddic poems that divulge the poetic intricacies of Norse mythology and history to the contemporary novels and TV shows that enthrall audiences with riveting tales from this era, the grandeur and spirit of Viking culture perpetually inspire creative minds. Notably, esteemed authors such as Frans G. Bengtsson and Jan Guillou have played a pivotal role in introducing the Viking legacy to a wider, more diverse audience, while the immensely popular Vikings TV series has successfully captivated global viewers, delving into the dramatic intricacies and profound complexity of the Viking way of life. Moreover, even contemporary artists, astutely recognizing the enduring allure of Viking symbols and motifs, adeptly weave these ancient aesthetic elements into their exceptional works, further immortalizing the symbolism behind Viking culture.

At the heart of this cultural admiration lies an intrinsic fascination with Norse mythology and history, which continues to resonate with audiences on a profound level. The Eddic poems, composed in the 13th century, provide invaluable insight into the ancient beliefs, valorous exploits, and mystical realms inhabited by the Norse gods and heroes. These timeless verses, narrating the tales of mighty gods like Odin, Thor, and Freyja, as well as the captivating adventures of legendary figures such as Sigurd and Ragnar Lothbrok, serve as the cornerstone of Swedish literature, and a testament to the enduring heritage of the Vikings.

Building upon the foundations laid by these ancient poems, acclaimed authors such as Frans G. Bengtsson and Jan Guillou rose to prominence, skillfully wielding their pens to bring the vibrant world of the Vikings to life for a wider audience. Bengtsson's magnum opus, the historical novel "The Long Ships," stands as a veritable masterpiece, expertly capturing the Viking spirit, unyielding ambition, and audacious seafaring endeavors that defined this fierce warrior culture. Immersed in a vivid tapestry of historical events, this epic saga follows the adventures of Red Orm, a fictional Viking protagonist whose exploits anchor the narrative, enabling readers to delve into the captivating world of the Vikings as if transported through time.

Similarly, Jan Guillou's illustrious career as a novelist and journalist provided a fertile ground for yet another eulogy to the Vikings. His sensational "Crusades Trilogy," comprising "The Road to Jerusalem," "The Templar Knight," and "The Birth of the Kingdom," skillfully interweaves history and fiction, as it captures the journey of Arn de Gothia, a fictional Swedish knight who becomes embroiled in the tumultuous events surrounding the Crusades. While Guillou's novels primarily address the historical context of the era, the underlying Viking influence remains palpable, forging a powerful connection between the ancestral heritage of the Swedes and the captivating allure of the

Viking era.

Expanding upon the literary realm, the small screen has proved to be an effective medium in introducing this captivating era to a global audience. The internationally acclaimed "Vikings" TV series, created by Michael Hirst, has attested to the widespread fascination with Viking culture, garnering immense popularity and critical acclaim. Launched in 2013, this chronicle of the Norse saga magnificently showcases the life and struggles of legendary figures, most prominently Ragnar Lothbrok and his sons, invigorating viewers with a visual feast of meticulously crafted historical settings, larger-than-life battles, and complex characters grappling with existential dilemmas. Through its compelling storytelling and engaging portrayals, the "Vikings" series not only bridges the gap between the modern world and the Viking age but also underscores the enduring appeal of this culture shrouded in myth and legend.

Beyond the realms of literature and television, contemporary artists have seized upon the timeless symbolism embodied within Viking culture, employing it as a rich source of inspiration for their works. Exquisite Viking symbols and motifs, such as the mighty Mjölnir hammer, the ferocious dragon, and the valiant Viking ship, continue to resonate with both creators and admirers of art worldwide. These emblems of strength, power, and adventure effortlessly find their way into paintings, sculptures, jewelry, and even fashion, adding a touch of the ancient and enigmatic to the contemporary artistic landscape. In doing so, artists pay homage to the intrepid spirit and indomitable legacy of the Vikings, ensuring that their symbolism endures, even in a rapidly evolving world.

The legacy of the Vikings continues to shape and define modern Sweden in countless ways. The values of courage, skill, exploration, and independence that were instilled by their Viking forefathers permeate every aspect of Swedish culture and national character. Through relentless efforts of preservation, exuberant festivities, and the creation of awe-inspiring artistic creations, the people of Sweden ensure that their Viking roots remain firmly planted in the fertile soil of history. Their spirit lives on, transcending time, inspiring future generations to embark on their odysseys of courage, skill, exploration, and independence.

The Viking Legacy

Economic and Trade Legacy

With their reputation as exceptional seafarers and traders, the Vikings built a formidable reputation in the 8th to 11th centuries. They established extensive networks that reached across not only Northern Europe but also Western Europe and beyond. As they explored new territories and engaged in commercial activities, the Vikings made an indelible mark on the lands and peoples they encountered.

Among the nations deeply tied to Viking heritage, Sweden stands out. Even in contemporary life and culture, Sweden retains strong connections to its Viking past. This is particularly notable in the realms of economics and trade, where the foundational routes established by early Swedish Vikings continue to shape business and prosperity in the modern nation. In this paper, we will delve into how Viking-era trade practices and routes have influenced modern Swedish commerce. Moreover, we will also analyze the significant economic impact of Viking heritage on Swedish tourism.

The Vikings' prowess as seafarers enabled them to traverse vast distances and discover new territories. Their voyages were not merely for exploration but also trade, as their ships carried goods that would fetch high prices in foreign lands. This emphasis on trade contributed to the establishment of a network of coastal and river routes that stretched from the Nordic region to as far as the Mediterranean. These routes were marked by the Norsemen's presence and became vital arteries for commercial exchanges.

The Viking presence in these trading routes left an indelible impact on the economic landscape of Northern Europe. The coastal and river routes provided opportunities for Swedes to engage in lucrative trade with neighboring countries. Timber, an abundant resource in Sweden, became a sought-after commodity, particularly in shipbuilding. The Vikings were quick to exploit this advantage, with Swedish timber becoming an integral part of their superior ship designs. This enabled them to dominate maritime trade and establish their reputation as formidable merchants.

The commercial influence of the Vikings extended not only to neighboring lands but also to more distant regions. They were among the first Europeans to establish contact with the Byzantine Empire and the Middle East. Through trade, they imported valuable goods such as silk, spices, and Islamic silver coins. This intercontinental exchange of goods enabled the Vikings to accumulate wealth, which subsequently fueled further exploration and trade ventures.

The foundations laid by the Vikings in terms of trade routes and commercial practices have had a lasting impact on Sweden's business landscape. Even today, the historical trade routes continue to shape the movement of goods and services within the country. The coastal regions, once bustling hubs of Viking trade, remain economically vibrant centers that foster commerce and industrial growth. The historical connection to maritime commerce continues to be a source of pride for Swedes, reflected in the nation's strong maritime industry.

Furthermore, the legacy of Viking trade practices is evident in Sweden's modern industries. Sweden is renowned for its innovative and globally competitive companies, particularly in sectors such as engineering, telecommunications, and information technology. The entrepreneurial spirit instilled by the Vikings, along with their focus on long-distance trade, continues to shape the business culture in Sweden. The nation's commitment to free trade and international cooperation can be traced back to the Viking Age when commerce was at the heart of their expansion.

The economic impact of Viking heritage extends beyond domestic commerce. Sweden's tourism industry significantly benefits from the nation's Viking legacy. Tourists from around the world are drawn to Sweden to experience the remnants of Viking civilization and immerse themselves in its rich history. The many Viking-era sites, such as burial mounds, ancient settlements, and historical artifacts, serve as potent attractions for visitors seeking a glimpse into the world of the Norsemen.

The allure of Viking heritage fosters cultural tourism in Sweden, bringing economic benefits to local communities and businesses. Museums dedicated to Viking history, like the Viking Ship Museum in Stockholm, attract countless visitors each year. These tourists not only contribute to the museum's revenue but also generate income for nearby hotels, restaurants, and transportation services. The economic impact of cultural tourism extends to various regions across Sweden, rejuvenating communities and creating employment opportunities.

Moreover, the popularity of Viking-themed events and reenactments adds another dimension to Swedish tourism. Festivals such as the annual Viking market in Birka recreate the atmosphere of an ancient Norse trading hub, attracting both domestic and international visitors. These events provide a unique opportunity for people to witness Viking traditions, crafts, and performances firsthand. The economic benefits of such events extend beyond tourism, as local artisans and vendors profit from the increased demand for Viking-themed products.

Recognizing the economic potential of their Viking heritage, Sweden has made efforts to preserve and promote this part of its cultural identity. Government initiatives have been implemented to support archaeological research, restoration of historical sites, and the development of tourist infrastructure. Collaboration between academic institutions, museums, and tourism authorities ensures the preservation and dissemination of knowledge about the Vikings. Consequently, the economic impact of Viking heritage in Sweden is not only immediate but also sustainable for future generations.

The mastery of the seas held by the Vikings, those intrepid Scandinavian warriors, sailors, and traders, is a testament to their remarkable capabilities as sailors and navigators. No doubt fascinating is the intricate web of trade networks that they established throughout the vast expanses of Northern Europe and well beyond its borders. Of particular significance are the Swedish

Vikings, who played an eminent role in the development of these early trade routes, connecting their homeland to distant and exotic lands.

These adventurous Swedish Vikings crafted major routes that stretched southward and westward, reaching as far as the shores of England, France, Spain, Portugal, the Mediterranean, and even North Africa. Their maritime prowess allowed them to venture forth into the unknown, where they established vital trade connections, often superseding those of other European powers. Just as the mighty longships of the Vikings cut through the waves with persistence and resilience, so too did the Swedish Vikings navigate through the choppy waters of trade, securing links that spanned vast distances and connected diverse civilizations.

Carrying the banner of Swedish exceptionalism, the Vikings from this Scandinavian land also forged important east-west routes. These routes facilitated the exchange of goods, ideas, and cultural influences with a wide array of destinations. The vast expanse of the Kievan Rus' became a site of vibrant trade activity with the Swedish Vikings, who journeyed into these eastern territories and fostered prosperous relationships. To the north, the Baltic states eagerly awaited the arrival of Swedish Viking traders, who brought with them commodities and luxuries from the lands of the West. Poland and Germany, in turn, looked towards the horizon, anticipating the arrival of ships laden with wares and treasures from far-off lands, carried by these enterprising Swedish mariners.

Yet, the reach of the Swedish Vikings extended even beyond these regions. Their insatiable thirst for exploration and commerce led them to venture into territories unfamiliar to their contemporaries. In their pursuit of prosperity, they sailed further, charting new trade routes and engaging with civilizations that previously fell beyond the purview of European merchants. Thus, the influence of the Swedish Vikings was felt in lands as diverse as the Byzantine Empire, the Middle East, and even parts of Africa. Their reputation as skilled traders, unmatched navigators, and fierce warriors transcended borders, reaching even the farthest corners of the known world.

To truly comprehend the significance of these complex

trade networks established by the Swedish Vikings, one must delve into the factors that fueled their ambitions and facilitated their success. Among these factors, three stand out as critical pillars upon which their impressive achievements rested: natural resources, advanced seafaring skills, and a quest for prosperity.

Sweden's bountiful natural resources, ranging from timber to iron ore, created a solid foundation upon which Viking trade flourished. With access to an abundance of raw materials, the Swedish Vikings possessed valuable commodities that were highly sought after by distant lands. Their magnificent longships, crafted from sturdy Swedish timber, stood as a testament to their mastery of shipbuilding techniques. These vessels, distinguished by their sleek and agile design, allowed the Swedish Vikings to navigate even the most treacherous waters with relative ease. Coupled with their navigational prowess, honed through years of experience, they possessed the means to explore uncharted territories and establish their presence in far-flung lands.

Fueling their audacious endeavors was an indomitable spirit of adventure and an unwavering determination to seek out new horizons. The Swedish Vikings, not content with the familiarity of their homeland, possessed an insatiable curiosity that drove them to explore and connect with foreign civilizations. Their quest for prosperity and wealth was a motivation that propelled them forward, pushing the bounds of what was then known and venturing into the unknown. By traversing vast distances and traversing formidable waters, the Swedish Vikings demonstrated their indefatigable spirit, willing to take risks in pursuit of remarkable gains.

It is through the lens of these three pillars – natural resources, advanced seafaring skills, and an unyielding pursuit of prosperity – that the full scope of the Swedish Vikings' impact on trade routes becomes apparent. Their incomparable ability to navigate the seas and their desire to expand their economic reach resulted in the establishment of intricate networks of commerce that spanned continents. Recognizing the importance of trade in fostering cultural exchange, the Swedish Vikings became conduits of cross-cultural pollination, bringing with them not only goods but also ideas and knowledge. They acted as ambassadors of their own culture, facilitating the exchange of cultures, beliefs, and innovations between their homeland and the lands that eagerly awaited their arrival.

The interplay between the Swedish Vikings and the regions they encountered was not merely transactional; it was a multifaceted symbiosis that left an indelible mark on the course of history. As they traversed trade routes, the Vikings from Sweden encountered civilizations and societies that were vastly different from their own. This exposure to foreign customs broadened their understanding of the world and shattered preconceived notions, leading to a cultural awakening that resonated within their society. The transfer of ideas, technologies, and artistic expressions enriched both the Swedish Vikings and the regions they interacted with, becoming a catalyst for intellectual and artistic growth.

To fully grasp the impact of the Swedish Vikings, one must delve into their cultural legacy and the lasting imprints they left behind. The trade networks they established became conduits not only for goods but also for the dissemination of Swedish culture throughout the known world. The sagas penned by Viking writers, such as the renowned Snorri Sturluson, recounted the exploits of these intrepid traders and seafarers, immortalizing their achievements and ensuring their legacy endured through the ages. Through these literary works, the world glimpsed the audacity, resourcefulness, and resilience of the Swedish Vikings, forever etching their names in the annals of history.

The historical significance of Viking trade routes cannot be overstated, as they laid the very foundation for Sweden's exceptional prowess in modern maritime commerce. These intrepid seafarers, with their longships and daring spirit, ventured bravely into uncharted waters, charting paths that would be followed by countless future generations. Remarkably, many of the contemporary shipping lanes still in use today closely follow the very routes first mapped out by these audacious Vikings over a thousand years ago.

It is within this context that we can truly appreciate the

major Swedish ports that emerged as vital commercial centers, such as the illustrious Stockholm. Situated strategically at sites that served as bustling hubs for Viking trade, these ports not only facilitated the exchange of goods but also fostered cultural and intellectual intercourse that transcended geographical boundaries. Today, such rich maritime heritage continues to reverberate within the very core of Sweden's robust economy. Shipping, occupying a preeminent position, stands as an indomitable cornerstone of the nation's prosperity, with Sweden proudly ranking high globally in terms of merchant fleet size and seaborne trade volumes.

Swedish firms have deftly capitalized on their country's advantageous geographic position, nestled snugly between Europe and Asia. This ardent endeavor allows them to wholeheartedly embrace the spirit of the Vikings, utilizing established routes from the Viking era to facilitate modern international trade. These routes, hallowed in history, serve as conduits connecting diverse lands, cultures, and economies. It is through these maritime arteries that the spirit of exploration, adventure, and economic exchange persists, cementing Sweden's reputation as a respected powerhouse in the global trade arena.

For centuries, Sweden has fostered a tradition of maritime excellence, adhering faithfully to the indomitable spirit of the Vikings. Just as these intrepid sailors had their eyes fixed firmly on the horizon, Swedish seafarers of today, armed with the latest technologies and knowledge, navigate the vast expanse of the open seas with unwavering determination. The Viking spirit lives on, coursing through the veins of every Swede engaged in the maritime industry, propelling them, like their forefathers, towards new horizons and bountiful opportunities.

The strategic positioning of Sweden has played an instrumental role in its maritime success, allowing it to bridge the gap between Europe and Asia. This geographic advantage acts as a catalyst, inspiring Swedish firms to navigate these ancient trade routes, forming intricate networks of international trade. In doing so, they breathe new life into the historical importance of Viking commerce, weaving together a tapestry of global economic interdependence.

Sweden's maritime supremacy rests not only on its rich historical legacy but also on its unwavering dedication to excellence in shipbuilding, seafaring, and trade. The meticulous craftsmanship and engineering prowess innate to the Swedish people are exhibited in the unparalleled quality of their vessels. With cutting-edge technology and unparalleled expertise, Sweden continues to churn out innovative and efficient ships, ensuring its merchant fleet remains a force to be reckoned with on the world stage.

It is also crucial to acknowledge the multifaceted impact of the Viking trade routes on Sweden's economic landscape. Beyond the mere transfer of goods, these maritime pathways fostered cultural exchange and knowledge sharing. The Vikings were not mere pillagers and warriors; they were skilled merchants who recognized the transformative power of trade. Their commercial endeavors transcended the acquisition of wealth, laying the groundwork for cultural diffusion and intellectual growth.

This spirit of intellectual curiosity and cultural exchange has persisted throughout the ages, manifesting in the flourishing education and research sectors of present-day Sweden. Swedish universities and research institutions excel on the global stage, attracting students and scholars from around the world. This intellectual exchange, fueled by the historical legacy of Viking trade routes, continues to enrich Sweden's intellectual landscape, nurturing innovation and contributing to the country's overall prosperity.

While it may be tempting to view Sweden's maritime success purely through the lens of economic prowess, such a narrow perspective would do a disservice to the profound impact that Viking commerce has had on shaping the nation's identity. Trade, as propagated by the Vikings, is not simply a means to economic ends but a means to forge connections, promote understanding, and foster peaceful coexistence.

Sweden, with its deep-rooted maritime heritage, has embraced this holistic view of trade. It recognizes that economic prosperity is best achieved when it is harmoniously intertwined with cultural exchange, intellectual growth, and a shared global vision. By deftly leveraging its strategic geographic position between Europe and Asia, Sweden ensures that its maritime legacy serves as a beacon of hope, unity, and progress in the modern era.

Embedded within the cultural fabric of Viking society was a profound understanding of commerce and its potential for prosperity. These intrepid seafarers ventured forth, guided by their unwavering spirit of adventure, in search of untapped markets and bountiful resources. As they navigated treacherous waters and charted unknown territories, the Vikings fortified the very foundations of trade routes connecting lands from the British Isles to the Byzantine Empire. This pioneering spirit not only brought greater access to exotic goods but also placed Vikings at the crossroads of diverse cultures, inspiring a wealth of ideas, techniques, and inspiration to bring home.

However, it was not solely the act of exploration that distinguished the Vikings' economic prowess, but their exceptional skill in craftsmanship that set them apart from their contemporaries. Vikings were revered as masters of the forge, capable of forging weapons and tools of unmatched quality. Their metallurgical know-how and precision in shaping materials granted them a dominant position in the global market for metal goods. Furthermore, the Vikings' craftsmanship extended beyond the realm of weaponry, permeating into the creation of intricate jewelry adorned with splendid gems and the weaving of intricate textiles that bewitched onlookers with their intricacy and beauty.

It is impossible to overlook how the Viking legacy in engineering and design reverberates through the modern realm of Swedish business. Sweden has earned a well-deserved reputation for its commitment to excellence and innovation in these fields. From the sleek minimalism of Swedish furniture designs, such as those by companies like IKEA, to the cutting-edge engineering marvels that populate the skyline of Stockholm, the echoes of Viking craftsmanship resound throughout the nation. The meticulous attention to detail, the appreciation for functionality, and the devotion to quality — all intrinsic values nurtured by the Vikings — enkindle the spirit of Swedish engineering and design.

This extraordinary continuum of Viking practices is especially evident when scrutinizing Sweden's contemporary manufacturing and export industries. The singularity of Viking craftsmanship, coupled with an unwavering commitment to precision, permeates the realm of Swedish exports. From automobiles to precision tools, Swedish products are heralded for their exceptional quality, unmatched durability, and unrivaled design. The knights of the Viking age, who set sail with swords at their sides, would surely be astounded by the technological marvels forged by their descendants. Yet, the relentless pursuit of excellence ingrained by their Viking forebears continues to fuel Sweden's relentless drive to push boundaries, constantly redefining what is achievable.

Moreover, the influence of Vikings on Swedish business culture extends beyond the tangible aspects of manufacturing and export. A sense of adventure and risk-taking, imprinted upon the Viking DNA, courses through the veins of Swedish entrepreneurs, propelling them toward unchartered territories and new opportunities. With their audacious determination, these modern-day explorers fearlessly tackle the global market, forging connections and alliances that perpetuate the entrepreneurial spirit of their Viking progenitors.

Yet, as with any narrative, shadows stalk alongside the tales of triumph and accomplishment. The Viking heritage of conquest and plunder is not without its implications for Swedish business culture. Just as the

Vikings sought to expand their economic reach through force, so too do certain Swedish companies occasionally find themselves tangled in the webs of controversy and ethical debates. However, it is essential to approach such discussions with nuance and recognize that the actions of a few do not define an entire nation or its identity. The Vikings' influence on Swedish business culture should be celebrated for the positive values it instills while acknowledging and mitigating the darker aspects that occasionally emerge.

Ultimately, the saga of the Vikings and their profound impact on economic practices and business culture in Sweden is an inextricable part of the nation's identity. The relentless spirit of adventure that resided within the soul of these Scandinavian warriors, coupled with their unrivaled craftsmanship, set the stage for Sweden to become a global powerhouse in engineering and design. As Viking longships once braved treacherous waters, so too do Swedish businesses navigate the ever-changing tides of international trade. It is through the lens of the Viking legacy that we can gain a deeper understanding of the values, skills, and mindset that continue to propel Sweden's economic success in the modern era.

The Vikings were not only fierce warriors and explorers but also astute economic practitioners. They developed advanced cooperative economic models that supported their extensive trade networks, which spanned across vast distances. Their key innovation in this regard was the development of early forms of partnerships and corporations that allowed groups to pool resources and share risks over long sea voyages. This cooperative approach, rooted in Viking culture, continues to influence the contemporary Swedish business landscape, where collaboration, consensus-building, and egalitarian work environments hold paramount importance.

The cooperative economic models adopted by the Vikings were instrumental in their success as traders. By joining forces, individuals and groups were able to leverage their combined resources and expertise, thus mitigating risks and increasing the chances of lucrative ventures. This collaborative approach allowed the Vikings to expand their trade routes, establishing connections with distant lands and flourishing economic hubs. In doing so, they not only amassed wealth but also facilitated the spread of ideas, knowledge, and technologies, thereby stimulating cultural exchange and intellectual growth.

Contemporary Swedish business culture still bears the imprint of this cooperative Viking legacy. The emphasis on collaboration and consensus-building is deeply ingrained in the Swedish work environment. This approach prioritizes teamwork, open communication, and a collective decision-making process. The typically flat organizational structures in Swedish businesses foster an egalitarian atmosphere, where every voice is valued and all members are encouraged to contribute their ideas and opinions. This collaborative ethos not only enhances productivity and innovation but also nurtures a sense of belonging and fulfillment among employees.

Furthermore, the Vikings' approach to trade was characterized by remarkable flexibility and adaptability. They recognized the inherent value of foreign goods, technologies, and ideas and were quick to incorporate them into their own culture and commerce. This receptive attitude towards new influences and a willingness to adapt has remained a defining trait of Swedish society and its economy. In the modern era, Sweden's remarkable economic success can be attributed, in part, to its innovative and export-driven economy. Swedish firms have demonstrated an ongoing ability to identify emerging trends and tailor their products and services to meet the needs of international markets.

The Viking legacy of openness and adaptability has fostered an environment in Sweden that encourages entrepreneurship and innovation. Swedish businesses, both large and small, actively seek out opportunities for growth and expansion in foreign markets. This enterprising spirit has led to the establishment of numerous successful Swedish multinational corporations known for their innovation and global reach. Notable Swedish companies, such as IKEA, Volvo, Spotify, and H&M, have built their international presence by understanding the needs of diverse cultures and adapting their products and marketing strategies accordingly.

Moreover, the adaptive nature of Swedish businesses extends beyond product development and marketing to encompass economic policies and practices. Sweden has consistently been at the forefront of economic innovation, with a strong focus on sustainability and social responsibility. The country has embraced renewable energy and environmental conservation, leading to the rise of green technologies and sustainable practices. Swedish companies are keenly aware of the global shift towards more conscious consumerism, and they have adapted their operations to meet these evolving demands.

In addition to embracing new influences and adapting to changing market trends, Sweden also has a history of fostering strong institutional support for business growth. The government, in collaboration with the private sector, facilitates research and development initiatives and invests in education and skill-building programs. Sweden's extensive welfare system and high-quality healthcare also contribute to a stable and productive workforce, which, in turn, enhances the competitiveness of Swedish businesses on the global stage.

The legacy of the Vikings is not confined to economic practices alone. Their rich cultural heritage, characterized by a spirit of exploration, resilience, and individual freedom, has left an indelible mark on the Swedish national identity. This cultural inheritance serves as a wellspring of inspiration for artists, writers, and thinkers, fueling the creative industries and contributing to Sweden's global reputation as a hub of cultural innovation.

The economic impact of Viking heritage tourism in Sweden cannot be overstated. From the ruins of ancient Viking towns to the carefully curated museums that house priceless artifacts, Sweden's Viking past has become a cornerstone of its tourism industry. This industry, in turn, drives economic growth and sustains thousands of jobs in the country.

Regions that were once home to Viking settlements, such as Gotland, Uppland, Södermanland, and Västergötland, have embraced their historical significance and developed a thriving tourism infrastructure. These areas have become magnets for visitors eager to explore the rich history of the Vikings and immerse themselves in the world of raiders and traders.

Among Sweden's most-visited attractions are the ancient Viking sites of Birka, Hedeby, and Gamla Uppsala. These sites offer a glimpse into the daily lives of the Viking population, revealing their economic practices, social structures, and cultural traditions. Tourists can walk in the footsteps of the Vikings, exploring the remnants of their settlements and marveling at the architecture and craftsmanship that defined their civilization.

Museums dedicated to preserving and displaying Viking artifacts have also become popular destinations for tourists. The Viking Museum in Stockholm and the Runestone Museum in Östergötland are renowned for their extensive collections of Viking relics. These artifacts provide valuable insights into the Viking era, showcasing the skills and ingenuity of these ancient craftsmen.

For those seeking a more immersive experience, places like the Foteviken Viking Reserve offer a unique opportunity to step into the Viking world. Here, visitors can participate in craft demonstrations, witness epic battles, and taste traditional Viking food. These experiences bring the Viking culture to life and create lasting memories for tourists from all corners of the globe.

In addition to historic sites and museums, Sweden also hosts various events centered around Viking culture. Larsfest in Söderköping, for example, celebrates Viking trade and seafaring, paying homage to the entrepreneurial spirit that characterized the Viking civilization. The Jamtamot Viking Market in Östersund, on the other hand, offers combat demonstrations, craft showcases, and authentic Viking cuisine. These events attract both locals and tourists, fostering a sense of community and cultural appreciation.

Another popular offering in the realm of Viking heritage tourism is the Viking heritage cruise. These cruises follow the routes once traversed by the Vikings, allowing travelers to experience the same majestic landscapes and seascapes that the Vikings once did. Such cruises provide a unique perspective on Viking history, connecting modern-day tourists to the seafaring adventurers of the past.

The economic benefits of Viking heritage tourism are substantial, as highlighted by a 2017 report. This report estimated that the industry contributes over 25 billion SEK annually to the Swedish economy, providing employment opportunities for tens of thousands of individuals (Visit Sweden, 2020). Regions that have invested in developing their Viking attractions have seen a noticeable increase in spending, job creation, and overall standard of living.

The enduring appeal of Viking heritage serves as a

major economic driver for Sweden. The ability to attract culturally interested visitors from all corners of the world is a testament to the enduring fascination with the Viking culture. Sweden's rich Viking history has created a unique niche in the global tourism industry, positioning the country as a must-visit destination for those seeking an authentic and immersive experience.

Sweden, a country steeped in Viking history, still maintains deep connections to its seafaring and trading past, even over a thousand years since the height of the Viking era. The extensive commercial networks and entrepreneurial practices established by early Swedish Vikings continue to shape the nation's strong position in global trade and business. Today, modern shipping lanes often follow the routes first charted by these seafaring explorers, while contemporary Swedish firms display an ongoing ability to produce high-quality goods, collaborate effectively, and adapt to international markets.

One of the most economically significant connections to the Viking past is the thriving tourism industry centered around Swedish Viking heritage and history. Throughout the country, numerous sites, museums, events, and experiences highlight this rich cultural legacy, attracting millions of visitors each year. Not only do these tourists contribute to the preservation and promotion of Viking history, but they also generate over 25 billion SEK for the Swedish economy. Regions with well-developed Viking attractions have seen increased prosperity due to the influx of tourism and the subsequent boost to local businesses and economies.

The legacy of the Vikings can also be seen in the foundations of contemporary Swedish trade and business practices. The pioneering trade routes established by the Vikings allowed for the establishment of extensive commercial networks that still exist today. These routes not only connected regions within Sweden but also extended to other parts of Europe and beyond. The Vikings' ability to navigate treacherous waters and explore new territories allowed them to establish trade connections with distant lands, enabling the exchange of goods and ideas. These historical trade routes have now become the basis for modern shipping lanes, allowing for the efficient transportation of goods globally.

Furthermore, the entrepreneurial economic practices of the Vikings have also endured through the centuries. The Viking society was characterized by a spirit of exploration, innovation, and risk-taking. This entrepreneurial mindset continues to be exemplified by contemporary Swedish firms, who are known for their ability to adapt to changing market conditions and produce high-quality goods. The Vikings' emphasis on craftsmanship and their mastery of various trades, including metalworking, shipbuilding, and farming, laid the foundation for Sweden's reputation as a producer of high-quality products. Swedish companies today continue to prioritize innovation and collaboration, both within the country and on the international stage.

In addition to shaping the economy, Viking heritage plays a significant role in the tourism industry. The allure of experiencing Viking history and culture has drawn millions of visitors to Sweden, eager to explore the rich and fascinating past of these seafaring warriors. From visiting archaeological sites and museums to participating in reenactments and attending Viking-themed festivals, tourists are immersed in a world that harkens back to a bygone era. The revenue generated from this booming industry not only benefits the tourism sector but also trickles down to supporting local businesses, hospitality, and the overall regional economy.

Sweden's embracing of its Viking past is evident in the efforts made to preserve and promote Viking culture. Numerous archaeological sites have been excavated and preserved, allowing visitors to uncover the secrets of Viking settlements and gain insight into their way of life. Museums dedicated to showcasing Viking artifacts and historical narratives provide a deeper understanding of this fascinating era. Additionally, events and experiences such as Viking reenactments and historical festivals help to bring the Viking age to life, transporting visitors back in time and immersing them in the sights, sounds, and stories of the Viking world.

Overall, the influence of the Vikings on shaping

modern Swedish trade and business is profound and enduring. Their pioneering trade routes and entrepreneurial practices have laid the foundations for Sweden's strong position in global commerce. Their legacy continues to enable the production of high-quality goods, effective collaboration, and adaptation to international markets. Furthermore, Viking heritage has become a major driver of the tourism industry, attracting millions of visitors and generating significant revenue for the Swedish economy. The ongoing preservation and promotion of Viking culture ensure that their impact remains palpable, reinforcing Sweden's prosperity in the present day, over a millennium after the Viking era.

Disclaimer

The publisher and the author are providing this book and its contents on an "as is" basis and make no representations or warranties of any kind concerning this book or its contents. This is a work of nonfiction. No names have been changed, no characters invented, and no events fabricated.

Although the publisher and the author have made every effort to ensure that the information in this book was correct at press time and while this publication is designed to provide accurate information regarding the subject matter covered, the publisher and the author assume no responsibility for mistakes, inaccuracies, omissions, or any other inconsistencies herein and hereby disclaim any liability to any party for any loss, damage, or disruption caused by mistakes or omissions, whether such mistakes or omissions result from negligence, accident, or any other cause.

About the author

Maher Asaad Baker (In Arabic: ماهر أسعد بكر), is a Syrian musician, author, journalist, VFX & graphic artist, and director. He was born in Damascus in 1977. He grew up with a dream of being one of the most well-known artists in the world, and he has been working hard to achieve it ever since.

He started his career in 1997 when he was only 20 years old. He had a passion for technology and media, and he taught himself how to develop applications and websites. He also explored various types of media-creating paths, such as music production, graphic design, video editing, animation, and filmmaking. He was not satisfied with just being a consumer of media;

he wanted to be a creator of media.

Reading was another source of inspiration for him. He was always surrounded by books as a child, thanks to his father's extensive library. He read books from different genres, topics, and perspectives. He read books for knowledge, for wisdom, for entertainment, for enlightenment. Reading stimulated his imagination and curiosity. Reading also developed his writing skills.

He did not start writing professionally until later in his life, as he was busy with other projects and pursuits. But when he did start writing, he proved himself to be a talented and prolific writer. He wrote articles for various newspapers and magazines on topics such as politics, culture, society, art, technology, and more. He wrote books that were informative and insightful. He wrote books that were creative and captivating. He wrote books that were best-selling and award-winning.

He is most known for his book "How I wrote a million Wikipedia articles", where he shares his experience of being one of the most prolific contributors to the online encyclopedia. He reveals his methods, techniques, strategies, and secrets of writing high-quality articles on any subject in record time. He also discusses the benefits and challenges of being a Wikipedia editor in the age of information overload.

He is also known for his novel "Becoming the man", where he tells the story of a young man who goes through a series of transformations in his life. The novel explores themes such as identity, masculinity, self-discovery, love, loss, and redemption. The novel is based on his journey to becoming who he is today.

Copyright © 2024 Maher Asaad Baker